Government

Extension to A Guide to the Project Management Body of Knowledge

Government

Extension to *A Guide to the Project Management Body of Knowledge*

(PMBOK® *Guide)* – 2000 Edition

Managing Government Projects

Project Management Institute
Newtown Square, Pennsylvania USA

Library of Congress Cataloging-in-Publication Data

Government extension to A guide to the project management body of knowledge
(PMBOK Guide)--2000 edition: managing government projects.
     p. cm.
  "March 2002"
  Includes bibliographical references.
  ISBN: 1-930699-00-X
    1. Public administration. 2. Project management. I. Title: Government extension to A
guide to the project management body of knowledge (PMBOK guide). II. Project
Management Institute. III. Guide to the project management body of knowledge.
JF1351 .M345 2002
352.3'65—dc21   2002028713

ISBN: 1-930699-00-X

Published by: Project Management Institute, Inc.
         Four Campus Boulevard
         Newtown Square, Pennsylvania 19073-3299 USA
         Phone: 610-356-4600 or Visit our website: www.pmi.org
         E-mail: pmihq@pmi.org

10   9   8   7   6   5   4   3   2

Contents

List of Figures

Foreword

On behalf of the Project Management Institute (PMI®) Board of Directors, I am pleased to present PMI's first application area extension, the *Government Extension to A Guide to the Project Management Body of Knowledge – 2000 Edition (Government Extension to the PMBOK® Guide – 2000 Edition)*.

The *Government Extension to the PMBOK® Guide – 2000 Edition* is an important step in PMI's continuing commitment to define the body of knowledge supporting the project management profession, and to develop standards for its application. The dedicated volunteers who worked on PMI's Ethics, Standards and Accreditation (ESA) Project first distilled the project management body of knowledge in 1983. Building on that work, PMI published *The Revised PMBOK®* in 1987. The publication of *A Guide to the Project Management Body of Knowledge (PMBOK® Guide)* in 1996 and the *PMBOK® Guide* – 2000 Edition continued the evolution. Today the *PMBOK® Guide* – 2000 Edition is an *American National Standard* and the *de facto* global standard for project management.

It has been PMI's intent for many years to supplement the information in the *PMBOK® Guide* – 2000 Edition by providing both industry-specific extensions and practice standards. The *Government Extension to the PMBOK® Guide – 2000 Edition* is the first such application area extension. It describes knowledge and practices that are "generally accepted" for government projects most of the time. It is applicable to government projects at the national, state/provincial, and local levels.

Finally, I would like to thank the globally diverse project team, led by Nigel Blampied, P.E., PMP, who worked so diligently to bring this standard to fruition. I would also like to recognize the PMI Government Specific Interest Group for the support they provided Nigel. Dedicated and competent volunteers have always been the backbone of PMI's success, and this publication is yet another example.

Rebecca Ann Winston

Rebecca Ann Winston, Esq.
2002 Chair – PMI Board of Directors

Preface

It has been PMI's intent for many years to supplement the information in *A Guide to the Project Management Body of Knowledge (PMBOK® Guide)* by providing both industry-specific application area extensions, and practice standards. The *Government Extension to the PMBOK® Guide* is the first such application area extension fulfilling PMI's intent. This extension is a supplement to the *PMBOK® Guide* – 2000 Edition and should be used in conjunction with the *PMBOK® Guide* – 2000 Edition.

The *PMBOK® Guide* describes the "generally accepted" knowledge and practices applicable to most projects most of the time, upon which there is widespread consensus about their value and usefulness. The *Government Extension to the PMBOK® Guide* describes knowledge and practices that are "generally accepted" for government projects most of the time. As an extension to the *PMBOK® Guide*, there are limits on what can be included. These are:

Chapters 1 through 3 (introduction, context, and processes): Specific sections of these chapters describe features that are peculiar to government projects, otherwise you use the information in the *PMBOK® Guide* – 2000 Edition because it has equal value for government projects.

Chapters 4 through 12: Information is presented in one of two forms:

A. **Introduction:** Describes features of the chapter's subject matter that are peculiar to government projects.

B. **Level 4 items:** As is the case in the *PMBOK® Guide*, a level 4 item is designated by a four-number series, e.g., *11.5.1.10 Common risk causes*. In contrast, a level 3 item has three numbers, e.g., *11.5.1 Inputs to Risk Response Planning*, and a level 2 item has only two numbers, e.g., *11.5 Risk Response Planning*. Apart from the introductions, changes to Chapters 4 through 12 should be at level 4. (The first level 4 item in Chapter 4 is 4.1.1.1 *Other Planning Outputs*. The last level 4 item in Chapter 12 is 12.6.3.2 *Formal Acceptance and Closure*.) For each item:

- You may find no change to the information in the *PMBOK® Guide* – 2000 Edition and you will be referred back to the appropriate level 4 section of the *PMBOK® Guide* – 2000 Edition. (If there are no changes to any items below level 2, you will be referred back to the appropriate level 2 of the *PMBOK® Guide* – 2000 Edition, rather than going down to each level 4.)
- You may find additional discussion or information about the existing *PMBOK® Guide* – 2000 Edition level 4 item, describing features that are peculiar to government projects.
- You may also find new level 4 items that are peculiar to government projects that are not found in the *PMBOK® Guide*.
- And, finally, you may find that a particular level 4 item in the *PMBOK® Guide* – 2000 Edition does not apply to government projects.

Chapter 1

Introduction

A Guide to the Project Management Body of Knowledge[1] *(PMBOK® Guide)* –
2000 Edition describes the "generally accepted"[2] knowledge and practices
applicable to most projects most of the time. The *Government Extension to
the PMBOK® Guide – 2000 Edition (Government Extension)* describes knowledge and practices which are "generally accepted" for government projects
most of the time.

The *Government Extension* is a subset to the *PMBOK® Guide* – 2000 Edition. The *PMBOK® Guide* – 2000 Edition provides the foundation from
which this extension was developed. All references found within this document derive from the *PMBOK® Guide* and, therefore, should be used in
concert with this document.

This chapter defines and explains several key terms and provides an
introduction to the rest of the document. It includes the following major
sections:

1.1   Purpose of This Document
1.2   What Makes Government Projects Unique?
1.3   What Is Project Management?
1.4   Relationship to Other Management Disciplines
1.5   Programs of Projects
1.6   Spheres of Government
**1.7   The *PMBOK® Guide* – 2000 Edition Processes—Inputs,
        Tools and Techniques, and Outputs**

1.1   PURPOSE OF THIS DOCUMENT

The primary purpose of *A Guide to the Project Management Body of Knowledge* is "to identify and describe that subset of the PMBOK® that is generally accepted."[3]

Appendix E of the *PMBOK® Guide* – 2000 Edition describes application
area extensions. It says "Application area extensions are necessary when
there are generally accepted knowledge and practices for a category of projects in one application area that are not generally accepted across the full
range of project types in most application areas. Application area extensions reflect:

- Unique or unusual aspects of the project environment of which the project management team must be aware in order to manage the project efficiently and effectively.
- Common knowledge and practices that, if followed, will improve the efficiency and effectiveness of the project (e.g., standard work breakdown structures)."[4]

This is an application area extension for government projects. The key characteristics of these projects are listed in Section 1.2.

1.1.1 Why Is the Government Extension Needed?

Governments around the world spend vast sums of money on projects. These projects cross many industries. These industries include Aerospace and Defense; Communications Technologies; Design-Procurement-Construction; Environmental Management; Financial Services; Health Services; Information Systems; Oil, Gas, and Petrochemical; Utilities; Safety needs; Welfare; Socioeconomic; and many others. Government projects in each of these industries have some features in common with similar private sector projects, but there are also features shared by all government projects that do not occur in the private sector.

It is in the interest of every taxpayer and every citizen that their government projects be well managed.

1.1.2 What Is the Goal of the Government Extension?

The purpose of this extension is to improve the efficiency and effectiveness of the management of government projects. Given the size of the government sector, even a marginal improvement will have enormous benefits to the stakeholders.

1.2 WHAT MAKES GOVERNMENT PROJECTS UNIQUE?

This extension refers to projects that have two characteristics:
- They are controlled by *elected* governments.
- They are funded from *mandatory* taxes and fees.[5]

Each of these characteristics is discussed in the following section.

1.2.1 Elected Government

In an elected government, the voters elect representatives who meet, deliberate, and set rules. They may call these rules by several names. They include laws, statutes, ordinances, regulations, and policies. Figure 1-1 depicts the interrelationship between these rules and the various participants.

Representative bodies consist of several members, who deliberate together to reach a decision. Having several members serves as a protection to the voters, taxpayers, and other stakeholders. If several people must agree on a decision, it is more difficult to keep secrets. This makes it less likely that there will be fraud or abuse of power. In addition, having several members encourages debate and a thorough consideration of the issues, thus resulting in better decisions, again to the benefit of the stakeholders.

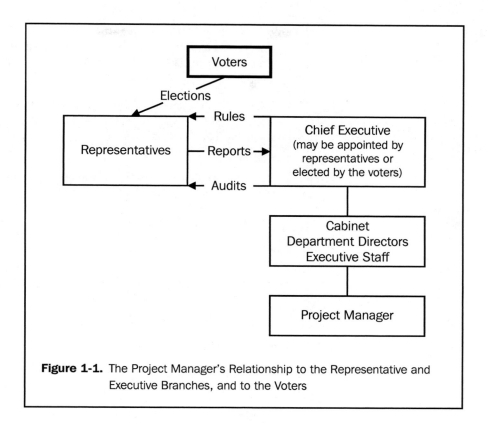

Figure 1-1. The Project Manager's Relationship to the Representative and Executive Branches, and to the Voters

It is generally not practical for a representative body to provide day-to-day direction to project managers. On projects, there are too many decisions to allow for group deliberation on every decision.

It is therefore necessary to have an executive who carries out the rules that the representative body has established. In most cases, the representative body appoints the executive. Sometimes, the voters directly elect the executive. There are also variations of the two approaches. Figure 1-2 gives examples of these variations.

An executive is necessary for efficient government, but the practice is fraught with danger. History has shown that people with too much power will abuse that power. Among their rules, the representative body must set clear limits on the executive. To proceed beyond those limits, the executive must obtain permission from the representative body, or from a commission or committee that acts for the voters.

To fulfill its duty to the voters, the representative body must require regular reports from the executive. It must also conduct audits and investigations to ensure that the executive is obeying the rules.

The most essential duty of the representative body is to produce a budget. The executive should not spend money without budgetary authority.[6] Without a budget, the government does not have the authority to continue functioning.

As they have responsibility for the day-to-day management of projects, project managers are part of the executive staff.[7] Most project managers report to members of the executive staff. On large projects or in small governments, they may report directly to the chief executive.

Executives appointed by the representative body: The Chancellor of Germany. The President of South Africa. City Managers, County Executives, and School Superintendents in the United States.

Executives elected by the majority party in the representative body and appointed by a ceremonial Head of State: The Prime Ministers of the United Kingdom, Italy, Sweden, Japan, the Netherlands, Canada, Australia, New Zealand, and India.

Executives elected indirectly by the voters, through an Electoral College: The President of the United States.

Executives elected directly by the voters: The Presidents of France, Russia, Mexico, and Brazil. The Prime Minister of Israel. Governors and some Mayors in the United States.

Figure 1-2. Examples of Appointed and Elected Executives, with Variations

---

1.2.2 Mandatory Taxes and Fees

In the private sector, people can choose not to buy a company's products. In government, people may be able to choose not to use a service, but they can seldom choose not to pay. If this is not balanced by an accountability system, it could reduce the motivation to perform well on government projects.

Accountability is greatest when people have the greatest freedom to vote. If many taxpayers are not allowed to vote, or if most voters do not pay a particular tax, there will be little motive for the representative body to hold the executive accountable for use of the tax.[8]

The project manager has a duty to use the taxpayers' funds to meet the goals set by their elected representatives.

1.3 WHAT IS PROJECT MANAGEMENT?

See Section 1.3 of the *PMBOK® Guide* – 2000 Edition.

1.4 RELATIONSHIP TO OTHER MANAGEMENT DISCIPLINES

See Section 1.4 of the *PMBOK® Guide* – 2000 Edition.

1.5 PROGRAMS OF PROJECTS

The *PMBOK® Guide* – 2000 Edition defines a program as "a group of projects managed in a coordinated way to obtain benefits not available from managing them individually."[9] Programs are more common in the government than in the private sector. Representative bodies in large governments generally assign funds to programs rather than to individual projects. This is because these representative bodies do not have time to consider individual projects. In small governments, on the other hand, the representative body may select individual projects. A local body may, for instance, vote funds for a new classroom at a local school. In the regional or national spheres, the representative body cannot consider this amount of detail. They vote a program of funds for school improvements, with rules for how the funds are to be divided among individual projects.

There are three methods that representative bodies can adopt for dividing program funds into individual projects:

- Delegate the decision to a commission. Commissioners are often nominated by the executive and approved by the representative body. Where executives are directly elected, the commission may consist of some members appointed by the executive and some by the representative body. Commissioners must have no financial interest in the projects and they often volunteer their time. Volunteer commissioners are paid only for their travel and accommodation expenses.
- Delegate or "devolve" the decision to a lower representative body. The national government might delegate decisions to regional or local governments. Regional governments might delegate to local governments.
- Delegate the decision to the executive. To prevent the executive from abusing power, this delegation must be subject to strict limits.

1.6 SPHERES OF GOVERNMENT

This document references three spheres of government:

- *National Government*. The government of an internationally recognized country. The country may be a confederation, federation, or unitary state.
- *Regional Government*. The government of a portion of a large country. In small countries, there are no regional governments—only a national government and local governments. In confederations and federations, the regional government has considerable autonomy. In unitary states, the regional government is subject to control by the national government. Regions are called by many different terms. These terms include states, provinces, lander, departments, cantons, kingdoms, principalities, republics, regions, and territories.
- *Local Government*. The government of a small portion of a country or region. There are often overlapping local governments with different duties. Local governments include counties, cities, towns, municipalities, school boards, water boards, road boards, sanitation districts, electrification districts, fire protection districts, and hospital districts. They are governed by elected boards. This election distinguishes them from local branches of regional or national governments.

1.7 THE *PMBOK® GUIDE* – 2000 EDITION PROCESSES— INPUTS, TOOLS AND TECHNIQUES, AND OUTPUTS

The *PMBOK® Guide* – 2000 Edition describes the inputs, tools and techniques, and outputs of each project management process. For each process, it includes a table that lists these elements. This document includes similar tables. In each table, the elements have this format:

■ Elements that remain unchanged from the *PMBOK® Guide* – 2000 Edition are shown in plain text.

■ New items are shown in ***Bold Italics***.

■ Changed elements are shown in *Italics*.

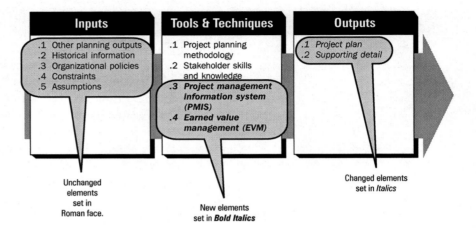

Chapter 2

The Project Management Context

The *PMBOK® Guide* – 2000 Edition advises that "Projects and project management operate in an environment broader than that of the project itself."[10] Section 2.1 describes some of the unique features of this environment for government projects.

2.1 PROJECT PHASES

A responsible representative body will require the executive to submit intermediate deliverables during project development. The phases of government projects often correspond to these deliverables. Government construction projects, for instance, typically have the five phases shown in Figure 2-1. Each phase in this example is required by a law adopted by a representative body.

2.1.1 Three Standard Phases

On many, perhaps most, government projects the main product of the project is purchased from the private sector. These projects have at least three phases.

- *Origination.* The origination phase is described in Section 2.1.2.
- *Planning and design.* This phase produces the documents that are necessary to proceed with the major procurement. They are described in rules established by the representative body. In the example shown in Figure 2-1, there are separate planning and design phases. If the alternative selection was straightforward, these could be merged into a single phase.
- *Procurement.* This phase acquires the main products of the project from the private sector. Procurement rules are established by the representative body. In the example shown in Figure 2-1, there are two procurement phases, one for real estate and the other for construction. In other government projects, there are activities outside the procurement for transitioning the project to the operational user, which can often be the point of failure for an otherwise successful project. This is particularly the case for complex Information Technology projects. For more information on procurement, see Chapter 12.

Origination
1. Origination document, used to obtain funding.

Planning and design
1. Alternative selection (planning), which is often controlled by environmental law. For example, on United States government projects, alternative selection is controlled by the National Environmental Policy Act.
2. Bid documents (design), controlled by public contract law.

Procurement
1. Property acquisition, using eminent domain law.
2. Construction, controlled by public contract law.

Figure 2-1. Typical Phases of a Government Construction Project

---

2.1.2 Origination Phase

Every government project begins with an origination phase. The product of this phase is called by many different names. These names include feasibility study report, basic planning report, project study report, project concept report, project location report, budget proposal, and funding request. It describes the product in sufficient detail to determine if the project should proceed. If there is a program of projects, the origination document is used to determine if the project should be included in the program. (For a discussion of programs, see Section 1.5.) If there is no program of projects, the representative body must approve each project separately. In this case, the origination document is submitted by the executive to request funding.

The budget must include some discretionary funds for the executive to produce project proposals. Without this funding, the executive cannot legally propose new projects.

2.2 PROJECT STAKEHOLDERS

The *PMBOK® Guide* – 2000 Edition lists key stakeholders on every project: the project manager, customer, performing organization, project team members and sponsor.[11] On government projects, the project manager, customer, and project team members are no different than for private sector projects. The performing organization is a department or agency that reports to the executive. The sponsor is either an executive official or a representative body.

Government projects have several other key stakeholders:
- *The public, including voters and taxpayers*. In addition to participation through their elected representative bodies, individuals and organizations may participate directly in a project through public hearings and reviews, as well as in lobbying efforts for and against the project, and for and against the various project alternatives.
- *Regulators*. The individuals or organizations that must approve various aspects of the project. Regulators enforce rules and regulations. They are actively involved in the project, but they generally have no interest

in its success—it will not affect them. Regulators are either agents of a higher government or of another agency in the same government as the performing organization. Thus:

- ◆ National government projects are regulated by other national government agencies. They are generally not subject to regulation by regional and local governments. National projects may also be regulated by international compacts such as the European Union, North American Free Trade Agreement (NAFTA), General Agreement on Tariffs and Trade (GATT), and Convention on International Trade in Endangered Species (CITES).
- ◆ Regional government projects are subject to the same regulation as national government projects. They are also regulated by other regional government agencies. They are generally not subject to regulation by local governments.
- ◆ Local government projects are subject to the same regulation as regional government projects. They are also regulated by other local government agencies.

Inadequate communication between the project manager and regulators can delay or even destroy a project.

- ▦ *Opposition Stakeholders*. Though not found in every project, this is a special class of stakeholders who perceive themselves as being harmed if the project is successful. An example is the homeowner who lives beside a park that is to be converted into a highway.
- ▦ *The Press*. In countries that have freely elected governments, the press is always present on major projects where large sums of money are involved. The press has a duty to report on the project in an objective manner, but often reports only the problems and not the successes.
- ▦ *Sellers*. In the procurement process, these are often significant stakeholders. They are discussed in Chapter 12.
- ▦ *Future Generations*. During their limited tenure, governments have a responsibility to future generations regarding long-term debt, viable and affordable infrastructure, and a viable environment.
- ▦ *The Private Sector*. The private sector provides counterpart funding and participates in public-private partnerships.

2.3 ORGANIZATIONAL INFLUENCES

See Section 2.3 of the *PMBOK® Guide – 2000 Edition*.

2.4 KEY GENERAL MANAGEMENT SKILLS

See Section 2.4 of the *PMBOK® Guide – 2000 Edition*.

2.5 SOCIAL-ECONOMIC-ENVIRONMENTAL INFLUENCES

See Section 2.5 of the *PMBOK® Guide – 2000 Edition*.

Chapter 3

Project Management Processes

Chapter 3 of the *PMBOK® Guide* – 2000 Edition describes five process groups:[12]
- Initiating processes
- Planning processes
- Executing processes
- Controlling processes
- Closing processes.

The application of these process groups to government projects is the same as in private sector projects.

Chapter 4

Project Integration Management

The *PMBOK® Guide* – 2000 Edition defines Project Integration Management as "the processes required to ensure that the various elements of the project are properly coordinated."[13] Chapter 4 of the *PMBOK® Guide* – 2000 Edition describes three major project integration processes:

4.1   Project Plan Development
4.2   Project Plan Execution
4.3   Integrated Change Control

In most cases, the application is the same in government service projects as in all others. In Project Plan Development and Integrated Change Control, however, there are significant additional considerations directly related to government projects.

In many instances, government projects and the priority accorded them result from policy requirements. This is not always the case, but when it is, project managers should be aware that the main objective is the implementation of the overall program, and not the execution of the individual project. This will require project managers to ensure that there is clear and continuing integration between the policy requirements, the program, and the project's scope and deliverables. Changes of policy might affect the program and, in turn, cause the project to be modified or even cancelled.

4.1   PROJECT PLAN DEVELOPMENT

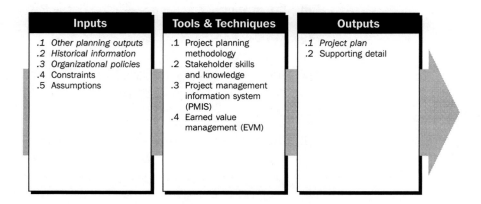

Inputs	Tools & Techniques	Outputs
.1 Other planning outputs .2 Historical information .3 Organizational policies .4 Constraints .5 Assumptions	.1 Project planning methodology .2 Stakeholder skills and knowledge .3 Project management information system (PMIS) .4 Earned value management (EVM)	.1 Project plan .2 Supporting detail

4.1.1 Inputs to Project Plan Development

Section 4.1.1 of the *PMBOK® Guide* – 2000 Edition discusses five types of inputs to Project Plan Development. All are used on government projects, and some have particular applications in government:

.1 Other planning outputs. Projects will, in some way, relate to the electoral cycle. Project managers should be aware of the significance of this cycle.

There is obvious pressure to demonstrate policy success by announcing "deliverables" from those contesting elections. There is the possibility of a reversal of policy should the administration change. Less obviously, there is often a principle of civil service neutrality during the electoral process that can require an avoidance of decision-making, which could be interpreted as favoring one party over another.

It is possible in a government structure, that the Program Office (which determines the need for a project to fulfill a mission) is separate from the Project Office (which executes a project). The project manager is often not involved in the programmatic discussions that take place, which can put the project in jeopardy. Once assigned, the project manager should open communications with the Program Office to ensure the project will satisfy the users' needs and will meet the technical requirements, if they change. Technical requirements often change as the administration changes.

.2 Historical information. Where the government body is the sole or dominant participant in the sector (for example, healthcare in the United Kingdom or defense procurement in most countries), changes in policy or methodology may invalidate local historical information. Indeed, the change may be intended to counteract a previous policy or methodology. Project managers should, therefore, be aware of the potential fragility of such historical information.

.3 Organizational policies. *Devolved powers:* As a general rule, public executive bodies only have such specific powers as the representative body gives to them. Actions outside these powers are *ultra vires* (beyond the power). For example, though a public body may own land on which to carry out its functions, it may not automatically have the power to sell, or benefit from the sale proceeds, of that land.

Approval controls: Different branches or tiers of government—local, national, and supra national (e.g., European Union)—may have separate formal requirements for approval of phases of the project. In principle, these are no different than the financial controls any organization would exert. Project managers should, however, make certain they understand the potentially diverse requirements for approval.

.4 Constraints. See Section 4.1.1.4 of the *PMBOK® Guide* – 2000 Edition.

.5 Assumptions. See Section 4.1.1.5 of the *PMBOK® Guide* – 2000 Edition.

4.1.2 Tools and Techniques for Project Plan Development

See Section 4.1.2 of the *PMBOK® Guide* – 2000 Edition.

4.1.3 Outputs from Project Plan Development

Section 4.1.3 of the *PMBOK® Guide* – 2000 Edition discusses two types of outputs from Project Plan Development. Both are produced on government projects, and one has particular applications in government:

.1 Project plan. The *PMBOK® Guide* – 2000 Edition discusses eight subsidiary management plans. Two of them, risk response and procurement, have particular applications on government projects:

- Scope management plan (*PMBOK® Guide* – 2000 Edition, Section 5.2.3.3).
- Schedule management plan (*PMBOK® Guide* – 2000 Edition, Section 6.4.3.3).
- Cost management plan (*PMBOK® Guide* – 2000 Edition, Section 7.2.3.3).
- Quality management plan (*PMBOK® Guide* – 2000 Edition, Section 8.1.3.1).
- Staffing management plan (*PMBOK® Guide* – 2000 Edition, Section 9.1.3.2).
- Communication management plan (*PMBOK® Guide* – 2000 Edition, Section 10.1.3.1).
- Risk response plan (*PMBOK® Guide* – 2000 Edition, Section 11.5.3.1). A key feature of governments is the presence of an opposition. Project managers should be aware that the project or the policy that causes the project to be is likely to be subject to actively hostile scrutiny from the opposition.
- Procurement management plan (*PMBOK® Guide* – 2000 Edition, Section 12.1.3.1). Government procurement is normally heavily regulated (see Chapter 12). This is to ensure equality of opportunity for applicants for public works and probity on the part of the procuring body. Where there is a choice of methodologies for procurement, that choice may determine the work and skills required of the project team. Project managers need to carefully consider the options available to them and the implications of following a particular route. For example, all public works and service contracts in the European Union (EU) above a certain value must be advertised throughout the EU, and can follow either a Tendered procedure or a Negotiated procedure. The latter would require a team with specific skills in negotiation to develop a contract and a price for the service or works required. If the needed negotiating skills were not available, an undesirable contract could result.

The *PMBOK® Guide* – 2000 Edition identifies that certain issues will remain open or pending. In government service, project managers should determine the body capable of resolving open issues, taking account of the legal powers of executives. At the highest level, this may require primary legislation—i.e., a new law—to be passed to enable the decision to be made. This is a lengthy process.

.2 Supporting detail. See Section 4.1.3.2 of the *PMBOK® Guide* – 2000 Edition.

4.2 PROJECT PLAN EXECUTION

See Section 4.2 of the *PMBOK® Guide* – 2000 Edition.

4.3 INTEGRATED CHANGE CONTROL

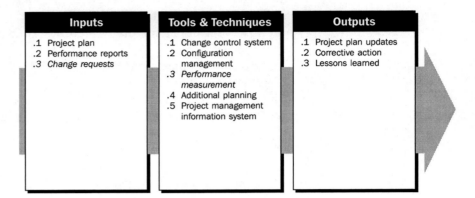

Inputs	Tools & Techniques	Outputs
.1 Project plan .2 Performance reports .3 *Change requests*	.1 Change control system .2 Configuration management .3 *Performance measurement* .4 Additional planning .5 Project management information system	.1 Project plan updates .2 Corrective action .3 Lessons learned

4.3.1 Inputs to Integrated Change Control

Section 4.3.1 of the *PMBOK® Guide* – 2000 Edition discusses inputs to Integrated Change Control. All are used on government projects, and one has a particular application in government:

.1 Project plan. See Section 4.3.1.1 of the *PMBOK® Guide* – 2000 Edition.

.2 Performance reports. See Section 4.3.1.2 of the *PMBOK® Guide* – 2000 Edition.

.3 Change requests. A major cause for the initiation of government projects is political policy. This policy is subject to change (e.g., a change in government or personnel in government). While not unique to government, such changes are usually publicly debated and well publicized in advance. The change is, therefore, a predictable consequence of a predictable event. Project managers should be aware of possible changes and plan accordingly.

4.3.2 Tools and Techniques for Integrated Change Control

Section 4.3.2 of the *PMBOK® Guide* – 2000 Edition discusses tools and techniques for Integrated Change Control. All are used on government projects, and one has a particular application in government:

.1 Change control system. See Section 4.3.2.1 of the *PMBOK® Guide* – 2000 Edition.

.2 Configuration management. See Section 4.3.2.2 of the *PMBOK® Guide* – 2000 Edition.

.3 Performance measurement. Performance measurement in government service is likely to involve independent scrutiny either by the representative body or by external bodies (such as the British National Audit Office or the United States General Accounting Office). In the former case, the scrutiny is as likely to focus on the policy underlying the project as on the plan to implement it.

Performance contracts for project managers and team members are becoming common. These contracts are linked to the relevant Key Performance Indicators of the specific program being managed.

.4 **Additional planning.** See Section 4.3.2.4 of the *PMBOK® Guide* – 2000 Edition.

.5 **Project management information system.** See Section 4.3.2.5 of the *PMBOK® Guide* – 2000 Edition.

4.3.3 Outputs from Integrated Change Control

See Section 4.3.3 of the *PMBOK® Guide* – 2000 Edition.

Chapter 5

Project Scope Management

The *PMBOK® Guide* – 2000 Edition defines Project Scope Management as "the processes required to ensure that the project includes all the work required, and only the work required, to complete the project successfully."[14] Chapter 5 of the *PMBOK® Guide* – 2000 Edition describes five processes:

5.1 Initiation
5.2 Scope Planning
5.3 Scope Definition
5.4 Scope Verification
5.5 Scope Change Control

Scope definition and management is often exceptionally difficult for government projects, since such projects frequently have many masters. The scope must not only satisfy the plans and objectives of the performing organization, but also the various regulatory organizations (see discussion in Section 2.2), some of which may provide portions of the project funds. The goals of these parties are sometimes in conflict. Thus, the project manager must take extra care to ensure that all parties are in agreement, to minimize problems downstream.

5.1 INITIATION

The *PMBOK® Guide* – 2000 Edition says, "Initiation is the process of formally authorizing a new project or recognizing that an existing project should continue into its next phase (see Section 2.1 for a more detailed discussion of project phases)."[15] It is important to remember that this process is repeated for each *phase*. An officer in the executive branch generally initiates the proposal phase. The initiation of later phases is determined by the rules set by the representative body (see Sections 1.2.1, 1.5 and 2.1).

The *PMBOK® Guide* – 2000 Edition lists typical reasons for initiating a project:

- A market demand
- A business need
- A customer request
- A technological advance
- A legal requirement
- A social need.

Each of these may occur on government projects, but they do not adequately describe the main reasons for initiating government projects. Government projects are initiated mainly for the health, safety, and welfare of constituents, and may address the following types of areas:

- Health needs (such as mass immunization, hospitals, sanitation, water purification, research, and food and pharmaceutical administration)
- Safety needs (such as defense, counter-terrorism, police, fire protection, disaster prevention and mitigation, prisons, justice, foreign policy, land mine inspection, and drug trafficking control)
- Welfare, socioeconomic, and environmental needs (such as participatory long-range planning projects, poverty alleviation projects, education and schools, water supply, transportation and roads, energy, social security, environmental protection, and parks and recreation).

Government projects may be initiated in order to achieve a specific policy goal of the administration, for example, a reduction in budget deficit, or the achievement of essentially political goals, such as the nationalization or privatization of utility companies.

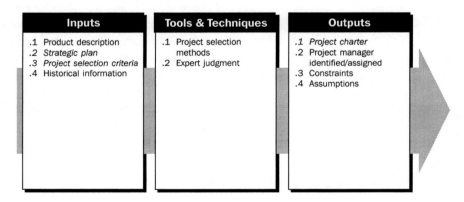

Inputs	Tools & Techniques	Outputs
.1 Product description	.1 Project selection methods	.1 Project charter
.2 Strategic plan	.2 Expert judgment	.2 Project manager identified/assigned
.3 Project selection criteria		.3 Constraints
.4 Historical information		.4 Assumptions

5.1.1 Inputs to Initiation

Section 5.1.1 of the *PMBOK® Guide* – 2000 Edition discusses inputs to Initiation. All are used on government projects, and some have particular applications in government:

.1 **Product description.** See Section 5.1.1.1 of the *PMBOK® Guide* – 2000 Edition.

.2 **Strategic plan.** See Section 5.1.1.2 of the *PMBOK® Guide* – 2000 Edition and the discussion of Quality Policy in Section 8.1.1.1 of this document.

.3 Project selection criteria. Section 5.1.1.3 of the *PMBOK® Guide – 2000 Edition* discusses the need to meet management concerns such as financial return, market share, and public perceptions. Government project selection criteria are characterized by nonprofit and socially driven characteristics that satisfy the needs and requirements of the constituents.

.4 Historical information. See Section 5.1.1.4 of the *PMBOK® Guide – 2000 Edition*.

5.1.2 Tools and Techniques for Initiation

See Section 5.1.2 of the *PMBOK® Guide – 2000 Edition*.

5.1.3 Outputs from Initiation

Section 5.1.3 of the *PMBOK® Guide – 2000 Edition* discusses outputs from Initiation. All are produced on government projects, and one has a particular application in government:

.1 Project charter. Section 5.1.3.1 of the *PMBOK® Guide – 2000 Edition* provides an outline of the requirements for a project charter. The charter of a particular phase of a government project is often included in the end product of an earlier phase. This is more apparent in government projects, as the new phase may include changes in executive responsibility, e.g., from the procurement arm to the operational arm.

.2 Project manager identified/assigned. See Section 5.1.3.2 of the *PMBOK® Guide – 2000 Edition*.

.3 Constraints. See Section 5.1.3.3 of the *PMBOK® Guide – 2000 Edition*.

.4 Assumptions. See Section 5.1.3.4 of the *PMBOK® Guide – 2000 Edition*.

5.2 SCOPE PLANNING

See Section 5.2 of the *PMBOK® Guide – 2000 Edition*.

5.3 SCOPE DEFINITION

See Section 5.3 of the *PMBOK® Guide – 2000 Edition*.

5.4 SCOPE VERIFICATION

See Section 5.4 of the *PMBOK® Guide – 2000 Edition*.

5.5 SCOPE CHANGE CONTROL

See Section 5.5 of the *PMBOK® Guide – 2000 Edition*.

Chapter 6

Project Time Management

The *PMBOK® Guide* – 2000 Edition defines Project Time Management as "the processes required to ensure timely completion of the project."[16] Chapter 6 of the *PMBOK® Guide* – 2000 Edition describes five processes:

6.1 Activity Definition
6.2 Activity Sequencing
6.3 Activity Duration Estimating
6.4 Schedule Development
6.5 Schedule Control

6.1 ACTIVITY DEFINITION

See Section 6.1 of the *PMBOK® Guide* – 2000 Edition.

6.2 ACTIVITY SEQUENCING

See Section 6.2 of the *PMBOK® Guide* – 2000 Edition.

6.3 ACTIVITY DURATION ESTIMATING

See Section 6.3 of the *PMBOK® Guide* – 2000 Edition.

6.4 SCHEDULE DEVELOPMENT

Inputs	Tools & Techniques	Outputs
.1 Project network diagrams .2 Activity duration estimates .3 Resource requirements .4 Resource pool description .5 Calendars .6 *Constraints* .7 Assumptions .8 Leads and lags .9 Risk management plan .10 Activity attributes **.11 Line-item projects**	.1 Mathematical analysis .2 Duration compression .3 Simulation .4 Resource leveling heuristics .5 Project management software .6 Coding structure **.7 Obligations**	.1 Project schedule .2 Supporting detail .3 Schedule management plan .4 Resource requirement updates

6.4.1 Inputs to Schedule Development

Section 6.4.1 of the *PMBOK® Guide* – 2000 Edition discusses inputs to Schedule Development. All are used on government projects. One input has a particular application in government and the last one is unique to government:

.1 Project network diagrams. See Section 6.4.1.1 of the *PMBOK® Guide* – 2000 Edition.

.2 Activity duration estimates. See Section 6.4.1.2 of the *PMBOK® Guide* – 2000 Edition.

.3 Resource requirements. See Section 6.4.1.3 of the *PMBOK® Guide* – 2000 Edition.

.4 Resource pool description. See Section 6.4.1.4 of the *PMBOK® Guide* – 2000 Edition.

.5 Calendars. See Section 6.4.1.5 of the *PMBOK® Guide* – 2000 Edition.

.6 Constraints. Constraints are described in Section 6.4.1.6 of the *PMBOK® Guide* – 2000 Edition. The *annual budget cycle* is the unique, and often most difficult, time constraint for government projects. To prevent the executive from abusing power, the representative body budgets funds for only a limited time. Budgets are typically for one fiscal year at a time.[17] This means that projects and programs must be divided into one-year slices. *Use it or lose it* provisions require funds to be spent by the end of the fiscal year. Project delays can cause the loss of funding if work moves from one fiscal year into the next. Fortunately, funds are generally appropriated to programs rather than individual projects (see Section 1.5). Effective program managers can often move funds between projects to minimize the overall loss of funding. However, some very large projects, in terms of their funding levels, keep their budgetary identity. No movement of funds to or from one of these projects can be processed without the clearance of the elected government or the individual(s) to whom the elected government delegates that authority.

.7 Assumptions. See Section 6.4.1.7 of the *PMBOK® Guide* – 2000 Edition.

.8 Leads and lags. See Section 6.4.1.8 of the *PMBOK® Guide* – 2000 Edition.

.9 Risk management plan. See Section 6.4.1.9 of the *PMBOK® Guide* – 2000 Edition.

.10 Activity attributes. See Section 6.4.1.10 of the *PMBOK® Guide – 2000 Edition.*

.11 Line-item projects. These projects are added to the budget by the representative body on a project-by-project basis. They often are not supported by a proposal from the executive (see Section 2.1.2). The representatives set their schedules and budget. As a result, these projects often have poorly defined scopes, inadequate funding, or unreasonable schedules. The project manager must expeditiously work with the customer to determine the scope of work and the appropriate acquisition strategy to accomplish the project within the time constraints.

6.4.2 Tools and Techniques for Schedule Development

Section 6.4.2 of the *PMBOK® Guide – 2000 Edition* discusses tools and techniques for Schedule Development. All are used on government projects; an additional tool is useful on government projects:

.1 Mathematical analysis. See Section 6.4.2.1 of the *PMBOK® Guide – 2000 Edition.*

.2 Duration compression. See Section 6.4.2.2 of the *PMBOK® Guide – 2000 Edition.*

.3 Simulation. See Section 6.4.2.3 of the *PMBOK® Guide – 2000 Edition.*

.4 Resource leveling heuristics. See Section 6.4.2.4 of the *PMBOK® Guide – 2000 Edition.*

.5 Project management software. See Section 6.4.2.5 of the *PMBOK® Guide – 2000 Edition.*

.6 Coding structure. See Section 6.4.2.6 of the *PMBOK® Guide – 2000 Edition.*

.7 Obligations. Obligations or encumbrances help to address the annual budget cycle constraint (see Section 6.4.1.6). They are useful on projects with large procurements, but can be used only if the representative body enacts rules to make them possible. As noted in Section 2.1.1, on many government projects, the main product of the project is purchased from the private sector. Some governments can obligate the funds for these contracts if the contract is signed before the end of the fiscal year. This obligation places the contract funds into a separate account that can be used only for the specific contract. The funds remain available for two to five years, depending on the rules set by the representative body. This avoids the need to vote funds in each fiscal year. It is a most useful technique on multi-year procurements.

Obligations are also used in inter-governmental agreements, sometimes called government transfer payments.

6.4.3 Outputs from Schedule Development

See Section 6.4.3 of the *PMBOK® Guide – 2000 Edition.*

6.5 SCHEDULE CONTROL

See Section 6.5 of the *PMBOK® Guide – 2000 Edition.*

Chapter 7

Project Cost Management

The *PMBOK® Guide* – 2000 Edition defines Project Cost Management as "the processes required to ensure that the project is completed within the approved budget."[18] Chapter 7 of the *PMBOK® Guide* – 2000 Edition describes four processes:

7.1 Resource Planning
7.2 Cost Estimating
7.3 Cost Budgeting
7.4 Cost Control

7.1 RESOURCE PLANNING

See Section 7.1 of the *PMBOK® Guide* – 2000 Edition.

7.2 COST ESTIMATING

See Section 7.2 of the *PMBOK® Guide* – 2000 Edition.

7.3 COST BUDGETING

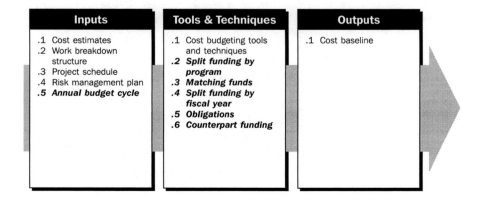

Inputs	Tools & Techniques	Outputs
.1 Cost estimates .2 Work breakdown structure .3 Project schedule .4 Risk management plan **.5 Annual budget cycle**	.1 Cost budgeting tools and techniques **.2 Split funding by program** **.3 Matching funds** **.4 Split funding by fiscal year** **.5 Obligations** **.6 Counterpart funding**	.1 Cost baseline

7.3.1 Inputs to Cost Budgeting

Section 7.3.1 of the *PMBOK® Guide* – 2000 Edition discusses inputs to Cost Budgeting. These are all used on government projects. A fifth input is of great concern on government projects:

.1 Cost estimates. See Section 7.3.1.1 of the *PMBOK® Guide* – 2000 Edition.

.2 Work breakdown structure. See Section 7.3.1.2 of the *PMBOK® Guide* – 2000 Edition.

.3 Project schedule. See Section 7.3.1.3 of the *PMBOK® Guide* – 2000 Edition.

.4 Risk management plan. See Section 7.3.1.4 of the *PMBOK® Guide* – 2000 Edition.

.5 Annual budget cycle. The annual budget cycle is discussed in Section 6.4.1.6.

7.3.2 Tools and Techniques for Cost Budgeting

Section 7.3.2 of the *PMBOK® Guide* – 2000 Edition discusses the tools and techniques for Cost Budgeting under a single heading. Several additional tools are used on government projects:

.1 Cost budgeting tools and techniques. See Section 7.3.2.1 of the *PMBOK® Guide* – 2000 Edition.

.2 Split funding by program. Programs are discussed in Section 1.5. Representative bodies in large governments generally assign funds to programs rather than to individual projects. They set rules for how the funds are to be divided among individual projects.

If the representative body budgets by program, each project must be funded from one or more of these programs. It is possible that a single project can contribute to the goals of more than one program. This is particularly common in transportation infrastructure projects. A road-widening project could be combined with pavement rehabilitation, bridge rehabilitation, seismic retrofit, or new signals. These are generally budgeted as separate programs. Similar situations are common wherever new facilities are budgeted separately from rehabilitation. It generally makes sense to have a single contractor perform both the new work and the rehabilitation at a particular location. This minimizes the overhead cost of developing and managing multiple contracts, and it minimizes the disruption to the occupants of the facility.

If a single project receives financial contributions from more than one program, it is *split-funded*. There are three possible methods of split funding:

■ *Defined elements of work*. Each program bears the cost of its portions of the project.

■ *Defined contribution*. Some programs contribute a fixed amount, with one program funding the balance. The balance is generally funded by the program with the largest contribution. This program bears the risks associated with cost overruns or underruns.

■ *Percentage split*. Each program funds a percentage of the project.

To the representative body, defined elements of work appears to be the best choice because each program pays only for the elements that it wants. However, this method requires a detailed manual accounting system, because an automated system can seldom discern which elements are being worked on. Such a manual process is prone to inaccuracy. It requires a large commitment of time for reporting and auditing. The increased cost generally outweighs the slight increase in the accuracy of charges.

The defined elements of work method also requires a far more detailed work breakdown structure (WBS) than the other two methods. To capture each program's portion accurately, the WBS must be defined to a level where each program's portion maps uniquely to a set of WBS elements. This level of detail is generally far greater than what is needed to manage the project.

The defined contribution does not require an amendment to the WBS. Typically, it is established as a "percentage split." When the limit is reached for the fixed programs, the split is changed to a 100 percent payment by the risk-bearing program. If the project is completed within budget, the change never occurs.

Percentage split is the simplest approach. The contribution of each program is estimated at the start of the project. Based on that estimate, each program bears its percentage of the project cost. As programs fund many projects, variances on one project will probably be counterbalanced by opposite variances on other projects.

.3 Matching funds. Matching funds are a form of split funding by program. When governments "devolve" project selection to lower representative bodies, they often require those lower bodies to pay a portion of the project cost. (See the discussion of devolution in Section 1.5.) This assures that the lower government is committed to the project.

Matching funds may be apportioned on a percentage basis or as a defined contribution.

.4 Split funding by fiscal year. The annual budget cycle is discussed in Section 6.4.1.6. If a project begins in one fiscal year and ends in another, it will need funding from the budget of each fiscal year in which there is project work. This split funding by fiscal year can be decreased through obligations, if the representative body allows them (see Section 6.4.2.7).

Funding by fiscal year requires that project managers plan their work by fiscal year with great care. This is particularly true in large governments with many levels of review. In the United States government, for instance, the President submits a budget to Congress in January for the fiscal year that begins on 1 October. Before this, the executive staff must assemble all the supporting data for the budget. Staff must also agree on priorities for the allocation of limited funds. To be included in the January budget, the project manager must have project plans completed by 30 June of the previous year. This is more than fifteen months before the start of the fiscal year. Once a budget request is submitted, changes are difficult to effect.

Fortunately, funds are generally appropriated to programs rather than individual projects (see Section 1.5). Program managers can use funds from projects that underrun their fiscal year budgets to fund the overruns in other projects. These are *fiscal year* variances, not variances in the total cost of the project.

Private sector firms could not survive with the government budget process. They must respond quickly to market challenges from their competitors. Without a quick response, they will lose business and may descend into bankruptcy. Large private firms, therefore, delegate the detailed budget decisions to smaller cost centers. The manager of each cost center has clear performance measures—make a profit, satisfy customers so that the firm gets return business, and obey the law. In government, there is no profit motive and customers seldom have the option not to return.

Paradoxically, fiscal year funding can have an effect that is opposite to what is intended. Annual budgets are intended to establish limits on the executive. In operational areas, they achieve this goal. (For a discussion of operations and projects, see Section 1.2 of the *PMBOK® Guide* – 2000 Edition.) On projects, they often fail. The executive must request budgets for each project in fiscal year slices. This focus on fiscal years can draw attention away from the overall multi-year cost of the project. The representative body may not see this overall cost. Projects can incur large overall cost overruns without the representative body becoming aware of this fact. Representative bodies need to be aware of this problem and require multi-year reports. Project managers should provide multi-year reports to their project sponsors.

Government accounting standards often fail to recognize the peculiar needs of multi-year projects. Project managers should keep records on the entire project that are reconciled with the government's official accounts.

Some governments have begun to adopt performance-based budgeting as an alternative to the rigid annual budget process. This is discussed in Section 8.1.2.6.

.5 **Obligations.** Obligations are discussed in Section 6.4.2.7. They are tools to minimize split funding by fiscal year. They can be used only where there is a contract with a private sector firm to provide portions of the product.

.6 **Counterpart Funding.** This is also called "counterfunding." It involves funding from the private sector, and is an option in "developing" countries, which will not have enough funds for many years to meet all the basic infrastructure needs of their population.

7.3.3 Outputs from Cost Budgeting

See Section 7.3.3 of the *PMBOK® Guide* – 2000 Edition.

7.4 COST CONTROL

See Section 7.4 of the *PMBOK® Guide* – 2000 Edition.

Chapter 8

Project Quality Management

The *PMBOK® Guide* – 2000 Edition defines Project Quality Management as "the processes required to ensure that the project will satisfy the needs for which it was undertaken."[19] On government projects, these needs are defined by the representative body, acting on behalf of the voters. In large governments, the needs are generally stated as goals for a program, rather than for individual projects. Each project must contribute to the program goals.

Chapter 8 of the *PMBOK® Guide* – 2000 Edition describes three processes:

8.1   Quality Planning
8.2   Quality Assurance
8.3   Quality Control

8.1 QUALITY PLANNING

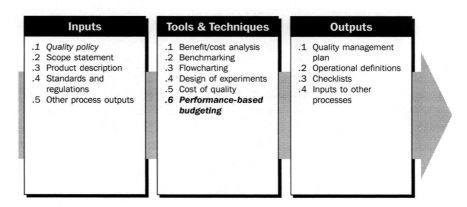

8.1.1   Inputs to Quality Planning

Section 8.1.1 of the *PMBOK® Guide* – 2000 Edition discusses inputs to Quality Planning. All are used on government projects, and one has a particular application in government:

.1   **Quality policy.** The *PMBOK® Guide* – 2000 Edition says, "Quality policy is the overall intentions and direction of an organization with regard to quality, as formally expressed by top management."[20] In government, quality policy is rooted in the constitution, the founding documents of the country, or in policies set by the representative body.

If quality policy is established in the constitution, the representative body will generally add further details in rules and regulations. The chief executive might add further refinements. Lower-level executives often add more refinements.

The *PMBOK® Guide* – 2000 Edition says, "The project management team is responsible for ensuring that the project stakeholders are fully aware of [the quality policy]."[21] On government projects, this means that they must be aware of their responsibilities under the constitution and under law (see Section 1.2).

Because government quality policy is rooted in the constitution and other documents that seldom change, government quality policies should not change much. Projects may vary considerably, but they remain focused on service to the voters and taxpayers.

.2 **Scope statement.** See Section 8.1.1.2 of the *PMBOK® Guide* – 2000 Edition.

.3 **Product description.** See Section 8.1.1.3 of the *PMBOK® Guide* – 2000 Edition.

.4 **Standards and regulations.** See Section 8.1.1.4 of the *PMBOK® Guide* – 2000 Edition.

.5 **Other process outputs.** See Section 8.1.1.5 of the *PMBOK® Guide* – 2000 Edition.

8.1.2 Tools and Techniques for Quality Planning

Section 8.1.2 of the *PMBOK® Guide* – 2000 Edition discusses tools and techniques for Quality Planning. All are used on government projects. A sixth one is also useful on government projects:

.1 **Benefit/cost analysis.** See Section 8.1.2.1 of the *PMBOK® Guide* – 2000 Edition.

.2 **Benchmarking.** See Section 8.1.2.2 of the *PMBOK® Guide* – 2000 Edition.

.3 **Flowcharting.** See Section 8.1.2.3 of the *PMBOK® Guide* – 2000 Edition.

.4 **Design of experiments.** See Section 8.1.2.4 of the *PMBOK® Guide* – 2000 Edition.

.5 **Cost of quality.** See Section 8.1.2.5 of the *PMBOK® Guide* – 2000 Edition.

.6 **Performance-based budgeting.** Sections 6.4.1.6, 7.3.1.5, and 7.3.2.4 discuss the problems of the annual budget cycle. Some governments have begun to adopt performance-based budgeting as an alternative to the rigid annual process. For projects, this is rooted in the concept of the *triple constraint*. Project quality is a combination of three factors—product scope, time, and cost. Quality projects deliver the required product scope on time and within budget. If a change is made to any of the three factors, at least one other factor must change. Every change is, therefore, a change in quality.

For programs and projects, the representative body establishes performance measures for each of the three quality factors. Program managers are permitted to trade off between the three factors to achieve the overall program goals. This includes permission to change the annual budget, within prescribed limits.

Performance-based budgeting can be of great benefit to the voters and taxpayers. However, there are pitfalls:

Performance measures must be carefully designed to encourage desirable behavior. Poorly defined measures can require managers to make the wrong decisions in order to meet their performance target. The design of the measures requires a thorough understanding of the program.

In large governments, the executive generally reports progress to the representative body only once a year. It would be wasteful to gather the data for more frequent reports, and the legislative cycle typically allows the representative body to take action only on an annual cycle. For performance-based budgeting, annual reports are inadequate. If performance is not adequate or the process is abused, the representative body must be able to take action more frequently than once a year. This typically requires an independent "watchdog" body, with paid auditors, which review data from the program and report to the representative body if there is a need to take immediate action.

8.1.3 Outputs from Quality Planning

See Section 8.1.3 of the *PMBOK® Guide* – 2000 Edition.

8.2 QUALITY ASSURANCE

See Section 8.2 of the *PMBOK® Guide* – 2000 Edition.

8.3 QUALITY CONTROL

See Section 8.3 of the *PMBOK® Guide* – 2000 Edition.

Chapter 9

Project Human Resource Management

The *PMBOK® Guide* – 2000 Edition defines Project Human Resource Management as "the processes required to make the most effective use of the people involved with the project."[22] Project Human Resource Management is one of the two *PMBOK® Guide* – 2000 Edition knowledge areas that focus on the acquisition and use of resources for the project. The other is Project Procurement Management (see the introduction to Chapter 12). All the resources used on a project are obtained either from inside the performing organization or they are obtained by procurement. The resources used on a project fall into four categories:

- Human resources obtained from outside the performing organization—discussed in both Chapter 9 and Chapter 12
- Goods (materials and equipment) obtained from outside the performing organization—discussed only in Chapter 12
- Human resources obtained within the performing organization—discussed only in Chapter 9
- Goods (materials and equipment) obtained within the performing organization.

Government agencies seldom produce the materials and equipment that are used on their projects. Their resource contribution consists mainly of human resources.

Chapter 9 of the *PMBOK® Guide* – 2000 Edition describes three processes:

9.1 Organizational Planning
9.2 Staff Acquisition
9.3 Team Development

9.1 ORGANIZATIONAL PLANNING

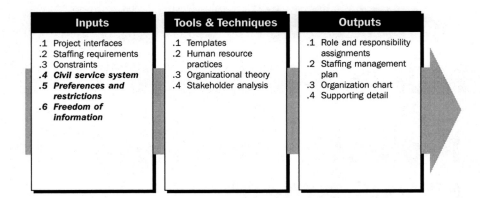

Inputs	Tools & Techniques	Outputs
.1 Project interfaces .2 Staffing requirements .3 Constraints **.4 Civil service system** **.5 Preferences and restrictions** **.6 Freedom of information**	.1 Templates .2 Human resource practices .3 Organizational theory .4 Stakeholder analysis	.1 Role and responsibility assignments .2 Staffing management plan .3 Organization chart .4 Supporting detail

9.1.1 Inputs to Organizational Planning

Section 9.1.1 of the *PMBOK® Guide* – 2000 Edition discusses inputs to Organizational Planning. All are used on government projects. Several additional inputs are used on government projects:

.1 Project interfaces. See Section 9.1.1.1 of the *PMBOK® Guide* – 2000 Edition.

.2 Staffing requirements. See Section 9.1.1.2 of the *PMBOK® Guide* – 2000 Edition.

.3 Constraints. See Section 9.1.1.3 of the *PMBOK® Guide* – 2000 Edition.

.4 Civil service system. The civil service system distinguishes government human resource management from that in the private sector. In an elected government, there is a likelihood that government policies will change from one election to another. Government employees must often implement policies that directly contradict those of a prior administration. In the past, this was often addressed by a "spoils system," where each new administration replaced government employees *en masse*. This system has been replaced around the world by a merit-based civil service. Civil servants hold office from one administration to another, but they must remain politically neutral. They are legally and ethically required to carry out the will of the voters, no matter how they feel. In many countries, civil servants may not be members of political parties or engage in any political activity other than exercising their vote.

As a guarantee of their neutrality, civil servants have tenure in their positions. Executives cannot remove a civil servant without documented cause. This can become a significant issue in establishing a project team. Each civil servant's position must be preserved. Assigning a civil servant to a position that is perceived to be inferior might be a *constructive demotion*.

Budget and law control civil service employee numbers. A project manager is not afforded the ability to hire personnel to fill critical skills needs (such as project controls), without going through a bureaucratic process. If a hiring is authorized, the process can take several months. Because project managers do not choose their staff, the project manager must create a viable, performing team from what is given. Project managers need to master teambuilding skills, understand the different personality types, and motivate these individuals to produce a functioning team.

.5 Preferences and restrictions. Governments will often give employment preferences to particular population groups. These may be ethnic groups, people who are deemed to be disadvantaged (e.g., women and disabled people), people to whom the voters feel indebted (e.g., military veterans), or citizens. There may also be restrictions based on security requirements.

.6 Freedom of information. See Section 10.1.1.5. Project managers might find themselves required to make public memos from meetings in which appraisals of staff performance or interpersonal problems were discussed.

9.1.2 Tools and Techniques for Organizational Planning

See Section 9.1.2 of the *PMBOK® Guide* – 2000 Edition.

9.1.3 Outputs from Organizational Planning

See Section 9.1.3 of the *PMBOK® Guide* – 2000 Edition.

9.2 STAFF ACQUISITION

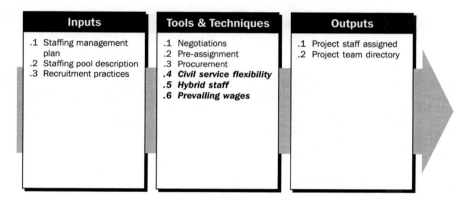

Inputs	Tools & Techniques	Outputs
.1 Staffing management plan	.1 Negotiations	.1 Project staff assigned
.2 Staffing pool description	.2 Pre-assignment	.2 Project team directory
.3 Recruitment practices	.3 Procurement	
	.4 *Civil service flexibility*	
	.5 *Hybrid staff*	
	.6 *Prevailing wages*	

9.2.1 Inputs to Staff Acquisition

See Section 9.2.1 of the *PMBOK® Guide* – 2000 Edition.

9.2.2 Tools and Techniques for Staff Acquisition

Section 9.2.2 of the *PMBOK® Guide* – 2000 Edition discusses tools and techniques for Staff Acquisition. All are used on government projects. Several additional techniques are also used on government projects:

.1 Negotiations. See Section 9.2.2.1 of the *PMBOK® Guide* – 2000 Edition.

.2 Pre-assignment. See Section 9.2.2.2 of the *PMBOK® Guide* – 2000 Edition.

.3 Procurement. See Section 9.2.2.3 of the *PMBOK® Guide* – 2000 Edition.

.4 Civil service flexibility. Although it is seldom recognized in formal human resource systems, more often than not, employees are able to choose among projects. Civil service makes this even more practical than in the private sector.

.5 Hybrid staff. It is common practice in government to contract for human resources using a contract form whereby the government pays the actual salary and overhead for such employees. While there is also a fee paid to the contractor firm, such employees are better described as hybrids between civil service employees and independent contractors. Such arrangements allow the agency to staff up and down for projects rapidly. Another rationale for use of such arrangements occurs in jurisdictions that are legally prohibited from recognizing employee organizations (unions). In many cases, such staff work in government-owned facilities and are managed by government employees. Project managers often supervise such staff much like other employees, with the exception of certain agency personnel systems.

.6 **Prevailing wages.** See Section 12.5.2.5.

9.2.3 Outputs from Staff Acquisition

See Section 9.2.3 of the *PMBOK® Guide* – 2000 Edition.

9.3 TEAM DEVELOPMENT

See Section 9.3 of the *PMBOK® Guide* – 2000 Edition.

Chapter 10

Project Communications Management

The *PMBOK® Guide* – 2000 Edition defines Project Communications Management as "the processes required to ensure timely and appropriate generation, collection, dissemination, storage, and ultimate disposition of project information."[23] Chapter 10 of the *PMBOK® Guide* – 2000 Edition describes four processes:

10.1 Communications Planning
10.2 Information Distribution
10.3 Performance Reporting
10.4 Administrative Closure

10.1 COMMUNICATIONS PLANNING

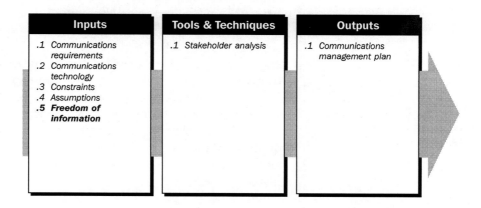

Inputs	Tools & Techniques	Outputs
.1 Communications requirements	.1 Stakeholder analysis	.1 Communications management plan
.2 Communications technology		
.3 Constraints		
.4 Assumptions		
.5 Freedom of information		

10.1.1 Inputs to Communications Planning

Section 10.1.1 of the *PMBOK® Guide* – 2000 Edition discusses four inputs to Communication Planning. All are used on government projects and they each have particular applications in government. A fifth input is also of concern on government projects:

.1 Communications requirements. Communications requirements unique to government planning are those based on information sharing in a functional bureaucracy. Government departments tend to be compartmentalized, not projectized. So when multi-agency communication will be required, how this will be accomplished should be planned into the project.

.2 Communications technology. The compatibility of technologies used to transfer information can vary significantly from one agency or sphere of government to another. The availability of funding for technology upgrades to mitigate communications inconsistencies should be factored into the communications planning.

.3 Constraints. A constraint likely in government projects is a lack of understanding about the communication process by the team members or their sponsor. Another constraint (though not necessarily unique to government projects), is the project manager's access to top management, especially during the "go/no go" decision gates.

In many government projects, contracted vendors/consultants (sellers) run the project day to day, reporting to an appointed government employee (project manager) who may have a limited project management background (or be selected as project manager based on technical expertise, rather than project management skills).

.4 Assumptions. The primary assumption is that the project team will be working with or for a governing body, its elected officials (in the case of a representative government), and its constituents.

.5 Freedom of information. Project managers may be constrained in what they may keep confidential. Public disclosure laws in many countries give citizens the right to view almost all governmental records, with a few non-absolute exceptions for secrecy and invasion of privacy.

10.1.2 Tools and Techniques for Communications Planning

Section 10.1.2 of the *PMBOK® Guide – 2000 Edition* discusses one tool for Communications Planning. This is used on government projects, and it has particular applications in government:

.1 Stakeholder analysis. Project stakeholders are discussed in detail in Section 2.2 of the *PMBOK® Guide – 2000 Edition*. Remember that not only the office holders but also the public (that is, the constituents, those governed, the taxpayers) are stakeholders. Timely and appropriate information needs to be clearly understood, therefore, by a broader range of affected individuals than is true for most private sector projects.

Analysis and planning to manage the information and consultation needs for all stakeholders can be beneficial in obtaining balanced outcomes. For publicly funded projects, accountability to the public and the openness of the political debate need to be factored in during project planning.

10.1.3 Outputs from Communications Planning

Section 10.1.3 of the *PMBOK® Guide – 2000 Edition* discusses one output from Communications Planning. This is produced on government projects, and it has a particular application in government:

.1 Communications management plan. On government projects, it may happen that government officials (rather than the project manager) control the communications. This could work well, but when it does not, it can become difficult to pinpoint the reasons for the communication breakdowns.

10.2 INFORMATION DISTRIBUTION

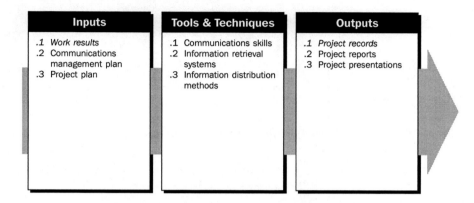

Inputs	Tools & Techniques	Outputs
.1 Work results .2 Communications management plan .3 Project plan	.1 Communications skills .2 Information retrieval systems .3 Information distribution methods	.1 Project records .2 Project reports .3 Project presentations

10.2.1 Inputs to Information Distribution

Section 10.2.1 of the *PMBOK® Guide* – 2000 Edition discusses three inputs to Information Distribution. All are used on government projects, but one has a particular application in government:

.1 Work results. Work results are described in Section 4.2.3.1 of the *PMBOK® Guide* – 2000 Edition. Reporting on the status of work and deliverables will vary from one jurisdiction to the next, and may be dependent on the procedures in the local, regional, national, or international spheres.

.2 Communications management plan. See Section 10.2.1.2 of the *PMBOK® Guide* – 2000 Edition.

.3 Project plan. See Section 10.2.1.3 of the *PMBOK® Guide* – 2000 Edition.

10.2.2 Tools and Techniques for Information Distribution

See Section 10.2.2 of the *PMBOK® Guide* – 2000 Edition.

10.2.3 Outputs from Information Distribution

Section 10.2.3 of the *PMBOK® Guide* – 2000 Edition discusses outputs from Information Distribution. All are produced on government projects, but one has a particular application in government:

.1 Project records. Project records may include correspondence, memos, reports (written or electronic), recorded records, presentations of content, and any other document describing and detailing the project. This information may become available to the public, or be made available via Freedom of Information Act requests (or similar legislation, depending on the government sponsoring the project).

.2 Project reports. See Section 10.2.3.2 of the *PMBOK® Guide* – 2000 Edition.

.3 Project presentations. See Section 10.2.3.3 of the *PMBOK® Guide* – 2000 Edition.

10.3 PERFORMANCE REPORTING

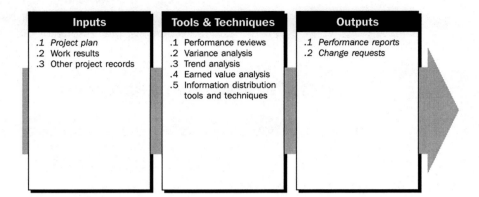

Inputs	Tools & Techniques	Outputs
.1 Project plan .2 Work results .3 Other project records	.1 Performance reviews .2 Variance analysis .3 Trend analysis .4 Earned value analysis .5 Information distribution tools and techniques	.1 Performance reports .2 Change requests

10.3.1 Inputs to Performance Reporting

Section 10.3.1 of the *PMBOK® Guide* – 2000 Edition discusses inputs to Performance Reporting. All are used on government projects, but one has particular applications in government:

.1 Project plan. The project plan is discussed in Section 4.1.3.1 of the *PMBOK® Guide* – 2000 Edition. It needs to account for any reporting on a project being performed on behalf of the government. Formats for this reporting may be prescribed by government components (such as defense or transportation), or have matching formats across all agencies.

Election cycles can influence the reporting timelines required by representative bodies and executives.

If the project is contracted, the vendors or consultants would likely submit project reports to the government employee project manager responsible for the work.

.2 Work results. See Section 10.3.1.2 of the *PMBOK® Guide* – 2000 Edition.

.3 Other project records. See Section 10.3.1.3 of the *PMBOK® Guide* – 2000 Edition.

10.3.2 Tools and Techniques for Performance Reporting

See Section 10.3.2 of the *PMBOK® Guide* – 2000 Edition.

10.3.3 Outputs from Performance Reporting

Section 10.3.3 of the *PMBOK® Guide* – 2000 Edition discusses outputs from Performance Reporting. Both are produced on government projects, and they have particular applications in government:

.1 Performance reports. Laws may prescribe the report timing and even the formats.

.2 Change requests. Significant sources of government projects' change requests are newly elected governments, oversight agencies, new rules, and new laws.

10.4 ADMINISTRATIVE CLOSURE

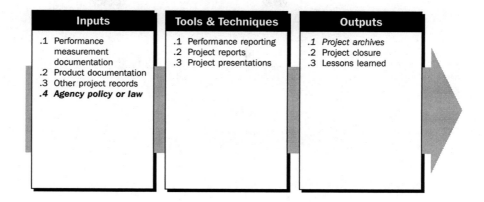

Inputs	Tools & Techniques	Outputs
.1 Performance measurement documentation .2 Product documentation .3 Other project records *.4 Agency policy or law*	.1 Performance reporting .2 Project reports .3 Project presentations	*.1 Project archives* *.2 Project closure* *.3 Lessons learned*

10.4.1 Inputs to Administrative Closure

Section 10.4.1 of the *PMBOK® Guide* – 2000 Edition discusses three inputs to Administrative Closure. All are used on government projects. A fourth one has particular importance on government projects:

.1 Performance measurement documentation. See Section 10.4.1.1 of the *PMBOK® Guide* – 2000 Edition.

.2 Product documentation. See Section 10.4.1.2 of the *PMBOK® Guide* – 2000 Edition.

.3 Other project records. See Section 10.4.1.3 of the *PMBOK® Guide* – 2000 Edition.

.4 Agency policy or law. This is especially important in regard to permanent archives described in Section 10.4.3.1.

10.4.2 Tools and Techniques for Administrative Closure

See Section 10.4.2 of the *PMBOK® Guide* – 2000 Edition.

10.4.3 Outputs from Administrative Closure

Section 10.4.3 of the *PMBOK® Guide* – 2000 Edition discusses outputs from Administrative Closure. All are produced on government projects, but one has particular applications in government:

.1 Project archives. Governmental record keeping is frequently defined by a myriad of laws and rules. Project records may need to be accessed years later, and by those unfamiliar with the project. Great care should be taken that the project archive is maintained for the required number of years, and in the required format as prescribed by governing records management standards.

.2 Project closure. See Section 10.4.3.2 of the *PMBOK® Guide* – 2000 Edition.

.3 Lessons learned. See Section 10.4.3.3 of the *PMBOK® Guide* – 2000 Edition.

Chapter 11

Project Risk Management

The *PMBOK® Guide* – 2000 Edition defines Project Risk Management as "the systematic process of identifying, analyzing, and responding to project risk."[24] Government risk is completely different from that in the private sector, except at the most basic level. At the basic level, all risk management has to do with survival. For a private firm, survival means that the firm remains in business. For elected representatives, survival means that they or their party remains in power. Loss of power is their greatest risk. Governments are replaced, but government very rarely ceases to exist. In the rare cases where there is a complete cessation of government (anarchy), people quickly form a new government.

Chapter 11 of the *PMBOK® Guide* – 2000 Edition describes six processes:

11.1 Risk Management Planning
11.2 Risk Identification
11.3 Qualitative Risk Analysis
11.4 Quantitative Risk Analysis
11.5 Risk Response Planning
11.6 Risk Monitoring and Control

Government projects follow the same processes, but their focus is on social, environmental, and political risk, as well as on financial risk. Many government projects would be abandoned if they were subjected only to the private sector risk analysis process. A well-known example is the program to place a man on the Moon and bring him back again. As a private sector project, this would have been completely unacceptable. It carried immense risks and had virtually no potential for profit. As a government project, however, it was an enormous success. (Success is judged by the stakeholders—in this case, the taxpayers and voters in the United States of America and their elected representatives.)

11.1 RISK MANAGEMENT PLANNING

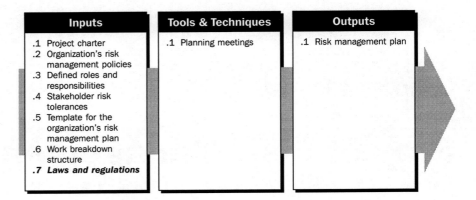

Inputs	Tools & Techniques	Outputs
.1 Project charter .2 Organization's risk management policies .3 Defined roles and responsibilities .4 Stakeholder risk tolerances .5 Template for the organization's risk management plan .6 Work breakdown structure **.7 Laws and regulations**	.1 Planning meetings	.1 Risk management plan

11.1.1 Inputs to Risk Management Planning

Section 11.1.1 of the *PMBOK® Guide* – 2000 Edition discusses six inputs to Risk Planning. All are used on government projects, and an additional input is of great concern on government projects:

.1 Project charter. See Section 5.1.3.1 of the *PMBOK® Guide* – 2000 Edition.

.2 Organization's risk management policies. See Section 11.1.1.2 of the *PMBOK® Guide* – 2000 Edition.

.3 Defined roles and responsibilities. See Section 11.1.1.3 of the *PMBOK® Guide* – 2000 Edition.

.4 Stakeholder risk tolerances. See Section 11.1.1.4 of the *PMBOK® Guide* – 2000 Edition.

.5 Template for the organization's risk management plan. See Section 11.1.1.5 of the *PMBOK® Guide* – 2000 Edition.

.6 Work breakdown structure. See Section 11.1.1.6 of the *PMBOK® Guide* – 2000 Edition.

.7 Laws and regulations. These are a particular form of the organization's practices and tolerances described in Sections 11.1.1.2 and 11.1.1.4 of the *PMBOK® Guide* – 2000 Edition. Voters, through their elected representatives, establish practices and tolerances for government projects. Some of these tolerances relate to:

- Air and water quality
- Affirmative action and assistance to disadvantaged groups
- Archeological, historical, and architectural preservation
- Assistance to small businesses
- Endangered species protection
- Noise prevention
- Religious freedom and the protection of places of worship and burial
- Protection of scenic areas and parks.

Several of these items are often combined into an omnibus environmental protection law. Although they generally do not use the word "risk," these are risk management laws. They inform the project manager of the limitations on the project and define risks that the voters will not accept.

11.1.2 Tools and Techniques for Risk Management Planning

See Section 11.1.2 of the *PMBOK® Guide – 2000 Edition.*

11.1.3 Outputs from Risk Management Planning

See Section 11.1.3 of the *PMBOK® Guide – 2000 Edition.*

11.2 RISK IDENTIFICATION

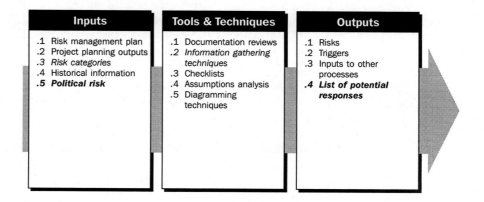

Inputs	Tools & Techniques	Outputs
.1 Risk management plan .2 Project planning outputs .3 *Risk categories* .4 Historical information .5 *Political risk*	.1 Documentation reviews .2 *Information gathering techniques* .3 Checklists .4 Assumptions analysis .5 Diagramming techniques	.1 Risks .2 Triggers .3 Inputs to other processes .4 *List of potential responses*

11.2.1 Inputs to Risk Identification

Section 11.2.1 of the *PMBOK® Guide – 2000 Edition* discusses four inputs to Risk Identification. All are used on government projects. However, risk categories have a particular application that warrants treatment as a separate input:

.1 Risk management plan. See Section 11.2.1.1 of the *PMBOK® Guide – 2000 Edition.*

.2 Project planning outputs. See Section 11.2.1.2 of the *PMBOK® Guide – 2000 Edition.*

.3 Risk categories. Section 11.2.1.3 of the *PMBOK® Guide – 2000 Edition* describes four risk categories:
- Technical, quality, or performance risks
- Project management risks
- Organizational risks
- External risks.

On government projects, one type of external risk far outranks all others. This is political risk. Due to its significance, it is treated below as a separate input.

.4 Historical information. See Section 11.2.1.4 of the *PMBOK® Guide – 2000 Edition.*

.5 Political risk. This measures the voters' opinion of the project. It could be considered a subset of "external risks" (Section 11.2.1.3), but to do so would decrease its prominence. The voters' opinion is the overriding concern on government projects.

A basic assumption in democratic societies is that the voters' decisions are correct. A government project manager is ethically bound to carry out the will of the voters, not to ignore or evade it. The will of the voters is displayed at the ballot box. It is conveyed to the project manager from the elected representatives through the executive.

There are many variations in voter opinion. These include:

- *Conflicts between voters in the national, regional, and local spheres.* Voters in national or regional elections, and their representatives, may support a project while local voters oppose the project. This is often associated with the NIMBY ("not in my back yard") phenomenon. National and regional voters may want a facility (e.g., a solid waste disposal facility), but local voters oppose it.
- *Inconsistencies in the will of voters.* For instance, voters may want to commute to work alone each day in their private cars, but also want to have no air pollution.
- *Changes over time.* Voters may support a project in its early stages, but oppose it later as its effects become better known.

11.2.2 Tools and Techniques for Risk Identification

Section 11.2.2 of the *PMBOK® Guide* – 2000 Edition discusses tools and techniques for Risk Identification. All are used on government projects, but one has a particular application in government:

- **.1 Documentation reviews.** See Section 11.2.2.1 of the *PMBOK® Guide* – 2000 Edition.
- **.2 Information gathering techniques.** Section 11.2.2.2 of the *PMBOK® Guide* – 2000 Edition discusses techniques for information gathering—brainstorming; the Delphi technique; and strengths, weaknesses, opportunities, and threats (SWOT) analysis. These techniques are the same for government projects, but the focus is different. On government projects, the focus of these techniques should be on the factors that are of concern to the voters and their representatives. Project managers should avoid the temptation to slavishly follow the factors that generally arise when these techniques are used in the private sector. In government projects, for instance, cost and schedule may be far less important than social factors like environmental protection and affirmative action.

  In addition to the techniques described in Section 11.2.2.2 of the *PMBOK® Guide* – 2000 Edition, field research and surveys can be most valuable on government projects:

  - *Field research* is essential in environmental areas such as air and water quality, the protection of endangered species, and noise prevention. Specialists need to perform field observations and tests to ascertain how the project might affect these factors.
  - *Surveys* are useful in measuring some of the social concerns of voters such as affirmative action, archeological, historical, and architectural preservation, and the protection of scenic areas.
- **.3 Checklists.** See Section 11.2.2.3 of the *PMBOK® Guide* – 2000 Edition.
- **.4 Assumptions analysis.** See Section 11.2.2.4 of the *PMBOK® Guide* – 2000 Edition.
- **.5 Diagramming techniques.** See Section 11.2.2.5 of the *PMBOK® Guide* – 2000 Edition.

11.2.3 Outputs from Risk Identification

Section 11.2.3 of the *PMBOK® Guide* – 2000 Edition discusses three outputs from Risk Identification. All are produced on government projects, and an additional output is of great concern on government projects:

.1 Risks. See Section 11.2.3.1 of the *PMBOK® Guide* – 2000 Edition.

.2 Triggers. See Section 11.2.3.2 of the *PMBOK® Guide* – 2000 Edition.

.3 Inputs to other processes. See Section 11.2.3.3 of the *PMBOK® Guide* – 2000 Edition.

.4 List of potential responses. The production of this list is one of the most creative parts of project management, and it is critical to the remainder of the risk management process. Effective risk responses can create "win-win" situations that satisfy several competing groups of stakeholders.

Consideration of potential responses begins in the scope planning process. Potential responses are closely related to, and often dependent on, alternatives identification (see Section 5.2.2.3 of the *PMBOK® Guide* – 2000 Edition).

"No go" is always a potential response. This may be called by a variety of terms, including "do nothing" and "no build." The product of the project must be perceived to have greater value to the voters than the sum of its economic, social, and environmental costs.

11.3 QUALITATIVE RISK ANALYSIS

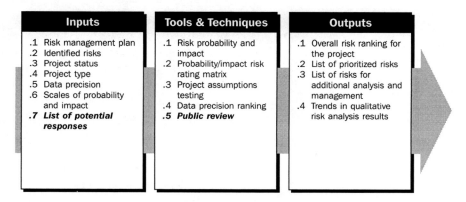

Inputs	Tools & Techniques	Outputs
.1 Risk management plan .2 Identified risks .3 Project status .4 Project type .5 Data precision .6 Scales of probability and impact **.7 List of potential responses**	.1 Risk probability and impact .2 Probability/impact risk rating matrix .3 Project assumptions testing .4 Data precision ranking **.5 Public review**	.1 Overall risk ranking for the project .2 List of prioritized risks .3 List of risks for additional analysis and management .4 Trends in qualitative risk analysis results

11.3.1 Inputs to Qualitative Risk Analysis

Section 11.3.1 of the *PMBOK® Guide* – 2000 Edition discusses six inputs to Qualitative Risk Analysis. All are used on government projects, and an additional input is of great concern on government projects:

.1 Risk management plan. See Section 11.3.1.1 of the *PMBOK® Guide* – 2000 Edition.

.2 Identified risks. See Section 11.3.1.2 of the *PMBOK® Guide* – 2000 Edition.

.3 Project status. See Section 11.3.1.3 of the *PMBOK® Guide* – 2000 Edition.

.4 Project type. See Section 11.3.1.4 of the *PMBOK® Guide* – 2000 Edition.

.5 Data precision. See Section 11.3.1.5 of the *PMBOK® Guide* – 2000 Edition.

.6 Scales of probability and impact. See Section 11.3.1.6 of the *PMBOK® Guide* – 2000 Edition.

.7 List of potential responses. The list of potential responses is described in Section 11.2.3.4.

11.3.2 Tools and Techniques for Qualitative Risk Analysis

Section 11.3.2 of the *PMBOK® Guide* – 2000 Edition discusses four tools and techniques for Qualitative Risk Analysis. All used on government projects, and an additional tool is most useful on government projects:

.1 Risk probability and impact. See Section 11.3.2.1 of the *PMBOK® Guide* – 2000 Edition.

.2 Probability/impact risk rating matrix. See Section 11.3.2.2 of the *PMBOK® Guide* – 2000 Edition.

.3 Project assumptions testing. See Section 11.3.2.3 of the *PMBOK® Guide* – 2000 Edition.

.4 Data precision ranking. See Section 11.3.2.4 of the *PMBOK® Guide* – 2000 Edition.

.5 Public review. If there is any controversy about a government project, it should be subjected to public scrutiny. This allows the elected representatives to gauge voter opinion. Some of the best practices in public review include:

- Helping opponents of the project to make their case. Every project has advantages and disadvantages. The opponents of the project need to have the opportunity to present their case in a clear, logical manner. Often the supporters of the project have more resources and information. This leaves the opponents to respond mainly on an emotional level. Emotions do not inform the voters or contribute to the search for the best solution. Project resources must, therefore, be committed to helping the opponents to articulate their case and place a logical choice before the voters and their representatives.

- Holding workshops rather than public hearings. In a workshop, the different aspects of the projects are described at booths or information stations. At several stations, there are recording devices for people to give their opinions. Members of the public move from booth to booth to learn about the project and present opinions. This gives everyone an opportunity to participate. In public hearings, by contrast, there is one public place where people can address the assembly. Participation in hearings is limited to those who feel strongly about the project or who enjoy public speaking. Most people do not participate. Workshops give a better gauge of public opinion and are more useful in developing logical arguments and alternatives.

11.3.3 Outputs from Qualitative Risk Analysis

See Section 11.3.3 of the *PMBOK® Guide* – 2000 Edition.

11.4 QUANTITATIVE RISK ANALYSIS

Quantitative risk analysis on government projects has similar processes to private sector projects. Unlike private sector projects, however, government risk is not expressed only in terms of cost and schedule. Social and environmental concerns often carry much greater weight than cost and schedule.

Inputs	Tools & Techniques	Outputs
.1 Risk management plan .2 Identified risks .3 List of prioritized risks .4 List of risks for additional analysis and management .5 Historical information .6 Expert judgment .7 Other planning outputs .8 **List of potential responses**	.1 Interviewing .2 Sensitivity analysis .3 Decision tree analysis .4 Simulation	.1 Prioritized list of quantified risks .2 Probabilistic analysis of the project .3 Probability of overrunning the project cost and time objectives .4 Contingency reserve amounts needed

11.4.1 Inputs to Quantitative Risk Analysis

Section 11.4.1 of the *PMBOK® Guide* – 2000 Edition discusses seven inputs to Quantitative Risk Analysis. All are used on government projects, and an additional input is of great concern on government projects:

.1 Risk management plan. See Section 11.4.1.1 of the *PMBOK® Guide* – 2000 Edition.

.2 Identified risks. See Section 11.4.1.2 of the *PMBOK® Guide* – 2000 Edition.

.3 List of prioritized risks. See Section 11.4.1.3 of the *PMBOK® Guide* – 2000 Edition.

.4 List of risks for additional analysis and management. See Section 11.4.1.4 of the *PMBOK® Guide* – 2000 Edition.

.5 Historical information. See Section 11.4.1.5 of the *PMBOK® Guide* – 2000 Edition.

.6 Expert judgment. See Section 11.4.1.6 of the *PMBOK® Guide* – 2000 Edition.

.7 Other planning outputs. See Section 11.4.1.7 of the *PMBOK® Guide* – 2000 Edition.

.8 List of potential responses. The list of potential responses is described in Section 11.2.3.4.

11.4.2 Tools and Techniques for Quantitative Risk Analysis

See Section 11.4.2 of the *PMBOK® Guide* – 2000 Edition. In Section 11.4.2.1, *interviewing,* note that project stakeholders are discussed in Section 2.2.

11.4.3 Outputs from Quantitative Risk Analysis

See Section 11.4.3 of the *PMBOK® Guide* – 2000 Edition.

11.5 RISK RESPONSE PLANNING

Inputs	Tools & Techniques	Outputs
.1 Risk management plan .2 List of prioritized risks .3 Risk ranking of the project .4 Prioritized list of quantified risks .5 Probabilistic analysis of the project .6 Probability of achieving the cost and time objectives .7 List of potential responses .8 Risk thresholds .9 Risk owners .10 Common risk causes .11 Trends in qualitative and quantitative risk analysis results	.1 Avoidance .2 Transference .3 Mitigation .4 Acceptance .5 *No go decision*	.1 Risk response plan .2 Residual risks .3 Secondary risks .4 Contractual agreements .5 Contingency reserve amounts needed .6 Inputs to other processes .7 Inputs to a revised project plan .8 *Work breakdown structure updates* .9 *Schedule changes* .10 *Cost changes*

11.5.1 Inputs to Risk Response Planning

See Section 11.5.1 of the *PMBOK® Guide* – 2000 Edition.

11.5.2 Tools and Techniques for Risk Response Planning

Section 11.5.2 of the *PMBOK® Guide* – 2000 Edition discusses four tools and techniques for Risk Response Planning. These tools and techniques are all used when analyzing social, environmental, and political risks. If any of them is adopted, the result is expressed through amendments to the project work breakdown structure and associated cost increases and schedule extensions. A fifth tool must always be considered on government projects:

.1 Avoidance. See Section 11.5.2.1 of the *PMBOK® Guide* – 2000 Edition.

.2 Transference. See Section 11.5.2.2 of the *PMBOK® Guide* – 2000 Edition.

.3 Mitigation. See Section 11.5.2.3 of the *PMBOK® Guide* – 2000 Edition.

.4 Acceptance. See Section 11.5.2.4 of the *PMBOK® Guide* – 2000 Edition.

.5 No go decision. If the adverse impacts of the project are greater than the benefit it produces, the project should be abandoned. Impacts and benefits are measured from the perspective of the voters and their elected representatives.

11.5.3 Outputs from Risk Response Planning

Section 11.5.3 of the *PMBOK® Guide* – 2000 Edition discusses seven outputs from Risk Response Planning. They are all produced on government projects. Three additional outputs are of concern on government projects:

.1 Risk response plan. See Section 11.5.3.1 of the *PMBOK® Guide* – 2000 Edition.

.2 Residual risks. See Section 11.5.3.2 of the *PMBOK® Guide* – 2000 Edition.

.3 Secondary risks. See Section 11.5.3.3 of the *PMBOK® Guide* – 2000 Edition.

.4 Contractual agreements. See Section 11.5.3.4 of the *PMBOK® Guide* – 2000 Edition.

.5 Contingency reserve amounts needed. See Section 11.5.3.5 of the *PMBOK® Guide* – 2000 Edition.

.6 **Inputs to other processes.** See Section 11.5.3.6 of the *PMBOK® Guide –* 2000 Edition.

.7 **Inputs to a revised project plan.** See Section 11.5.3.7 of the *PMBOK® Guide –* 2000 Edition.

.8 **Work breakdown structure updates.** If a risk is being avoided, transferred, or mitigated, this will require additional work packages. These must be amended into the work breakdown structure (see Section 5.3.3.1 of the *PMBOK® Guide –* 2000 Edition).

.9 **Schedule changes.** See Section 6.5.2.1 of the *PMBOK® Guide –* 2000 Edition.

.10 **Cost changes.** See Section 7.4.2.1 of the *PMBOK® Guide –* 2000 Edition.

11.6 RISK MONITORING AND CONTROL

See Section 11.6 of the *PMBOK® Guide –* 2000 Edition.

Chapter 12

Project Procurement Management

The *PMBOK® Guide* – 2000 Edition defines project procurement as "the processes required to acquire goods and services, to attain project scope, from outside the performing organization."[25] Project Procurement Management is one of the two *PMBOK® Guide* – 2000 Edition knowledge areas that focus on the acquisition and use of resources for the project. The other is Project Human Resource Management (see the introduction to Chapter 9). All the resources used on a project are obtained either from inside the performing organization or they are obtained by procurement. On most projects, internal resources consist mainly of human resources. The only project resources that are not covered either by procurement or by human resources are goods that are produced by the performing organization and used on the project.

On government projects, the performing organization is the responsible government agency (see Section 2.2).

Governments around the world invest enormous amounts of money in project procurement. In the United States alone, government procurement in the construction industry amounted to $180 billion in 1999.[26] To estimate the total government project procurement, one must add government procurement in other countries and expand to other industries, such as health and human services, aerospace, defense, environmental, financial, oil, gas, petroleum, utilities, and communications technologies.

This enormous flow of money creates large risks and responsibilities for safeguarding the public's interest. One problem is a huge potential for corruption. Civil servants who manage contracts regularly approve payments that are several times their lifetime income. Civil servants are also subject to political pressures from elected officials whose constituents may benefit from a government contract. A second type of problem is when the purchased goods or services do not fulfill the intended requirements because of poorly defined expectations, which lead to misunderstandings or opportunities for misrepresentation by the vendor. A third type of problem arises from restrictive procedures designed to prevent fraud and abuse, which make procurement a difficult, costly, and time-consuming process without commensurate benefits.

Avoiding these problems is essential for the efficient use of government resources and for maintaining public trust. Good Project Procurement Management gives government the tools for controlling these risks. Project Procurement Management should serve the following purposes:

- Provide an open, fair, and competitive process that minimizes opportunities for corruption and does not give subjective partiality to a specific vendor
- Avoid conflicts of interest or the appearance of a conflict of interest
- Establish an objective basis for vendor selection
- Obtain the best value in terms of price and quality
- Document the requirements that a vendor must fulfill in order to obtain payment
- Provide a basis for evaluating and overseeing the work of the vendor
- Allow flexible arrangements for obtaining goods and services in given circumstances, when those arrangements do not violate the other purposes of Project Procurement Management.

To be effective, Project Procurement Management must be part of other institutional arrangements to protect the public's interest. These include procedures to ensure that no one person can make large payments without verification, regular audits, public competition for contracts, and independent inspection of products received from contractors. It also includes public disclosure of statements of financial interest on the part of officials responsible for procurement decisions, and public access to records and documents.

Open, fair, public competition is particularly important. If all contracts are publicly advertised and the results are also public, losing contractors are less likely to challenge the selection process. Public exposure decreases the likelihood of corruption and helps assure the voters and taxpayers that their funds are being handled properly.

Chapter 12 of the *PMBOK® Guide* – 2000 Edition describes six processes:

12.1 Procurement Planning
12.2 Solicitation Planning
12.3 Solicitation
12.4 Source Selection
12.5 Contract Administration
12.6 Contract Closeout

12.1 PROCUREMENT PLANNING

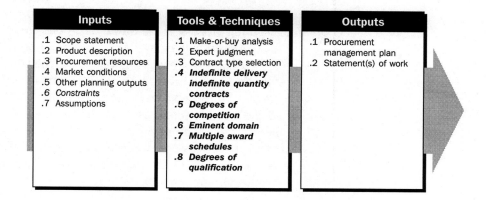

Inputs	Tools & Techniques	Outputs
.1 Scope statement .2 Product description .3 Procurement resources .4 Market conditions .5 Other planning outputs .6 *Constraints* .7 Assumptions	.1 Make-or-buy analysis .2 Expert judgment .3 Contract type selection .4 *Indefinite delivery indefinite quantity contracts* .5 *Degrees of competition* .6 *Eminent domain* .7 *Multiple award schedules* .8 *Degrees of qualification*	.1 Procurement management plan .2 Statement(s) of work

12.1.1 Inputs to Procurement Planning

Section 12.1.1 of the *PMBOK® Guide* – 2000 Edition discusses inputs to Procurement Planning. All are used on government projects, but one has particular applications on government projects:

.1 Scope statement. See Section 12.1.1.1 of the *PMBOK® Guide* – 2000 Edition.

.2 Product description. See Section 12.1.1.2 of the *PMBOK® Guide* – 2000 Edition.

.3 Procurement resources. See Section 12.1.1.3 of the *PMBOK® Guide* – 2000 Edition.

.4 Market conditions. See Section 12.1.1.4 of the *PMBOK® Guide* – 2000 Edition.

.5 Other planning outputs. See Section 12.1.1.5 of the *PMBOK® Guide* – 2000 Edition.

.6 Constraints. Constraints are described in Section 12.1.1.6 of the *PMBOK® Guide* – 2000 Edition. On government projects, most constraints revolve around the rules set by the representative body. These typically include:

- *An open, competitive process for selecting and awarding contracted services.* Competition is designed to ensure that the taxpayers get the best value. An open process is designed to prevent collusion and graft.
- *Standard evaluation methods*, published in advance.
- *The level of funding voted by the representative body.*
- *Programs to achieve social and economic goals.* These include preferences for disadvantaged population groups and preferences for small businesses.

.7 Assumptions. See Section 12.1.1.7 of the *PMBOK® Guide* – 2000 Edition.

12.1.2 Tools and Techniques for Procurement Planning

Section 12.1.2 of the *PMBOK® Guide* – 2000 Edition discusses three tools and techniques for Procurement Planning. All are used on government projects. Several additional tools are of particular use on government projects:

.1 Make-or-buy analysis. See Section 12.1.2.1 of the *PMBOK® Guide* – 2000 Edition.

.2 Expert judgment. See Section 12.1.2.2 of the *PMBOK® Guide* – 2000 Edition.

.3 Contract type selection. See Section 12.1.2.3 of the *PMBOK® Guide* – 2000 Edition.

.4 Indefinite delivery indefinite quantity contracts (IDIQ). Some agencies also call these *on call* contracts. Many agencies utilize this method of obtaining services for small projects. Open, competitive selection is a time-consuming process. To go through this process for each project would often cause unacceptable delays. IDIQ minimizes delay by performing the process once for many projects. In many cases, the contract is in place before the project starts. The contract states the type of service to be delivered, gives a length of time in which the service can be requested (generally five years), and the minimum and maximum contract amount. With this contract in place, a project manager can obtain architectural, engineering, or construction services without having to go through a separate solicitation process. This streamlined process supports small, non-complex projects.

.5 Degrees of competition.

- *Full and open competition.* All responsible sources are allowed to compete. This is the most used method of contracting.
- *Full and open competition after exclusion of sources.* Under this contracting method, agencies are allowed to exclude one or more sources from competing. A set-aside for small businesses or disadvantaged firms is an example of this method.
- *Other than full and open competition.* This is used when there is only a single contractor that can accomplish the work, by reason of experience, possession of specialized facilities, or technical competence, in a time frame required by the government. This type of contract is also known as "sole source," and requires a written justification to be approved by an authorized executive.

.6 Eminent domain. This is a particular form of sole source which falls in the category "other than full and open competition." It has been in use for thousands of years, and is probably the oldest form of government procurement. The government may take possession of private property when this is in the best interests of the public. Eminent domain is used most often to take possession of real property. The government is generally required to pay just compensation for the property. Such compensation is required in Roman Law, the Magna Carta, the Code Napoleon, and the Fifth Amendment of the United States Constitution.

.7 Multiple award schedules. In many jurisdictions, this type of contract is fairly new. It often requires specific legislation. It is used when there is a generally accepted "reasonable price" for a good or service. Contractors submit their schedule of rates to the government procurement office. If these are approved, government agencies may buy goods and services at the published rates without a separate competition. This method is often adopted in response to W. Edwards Deming's fourth point for management, "End the practice of awarding business on the basis of price tag. Instead, minimize total cost. Move toward a single supplier for any one item, on a long-term relationship of loyalty and trust."[27]

.8 Degrees of qualification. All government contracts require that the contractor have minimum qualifications that are listed in the solicitation documents. Once these minimum qualifications are met, there are several degrees of qualification that can be considered. There are some common approaches:

- *Lowest qualified bidder.* This is probably the most common approach. Contractors' proposals are evaluated to ensure that they meet minimum qualifications. Then, the cost proposals of the qualified contractors are opened and the lowest qualified bidder is accepted. The level of qualification may vary. On construction contracts, the minimum qualification is generally a contractor's license and a performance bond. On professional service contracts, there is generally a more detailed evaluation of the contractors' qualifications.

- *Weighted price and qualifications.* This process is similar to the lowest qualified bidder for professional services. Contractors are evaluated against several factors, with a pre-determined weight assigned to each factor. A weight is also assigned to the contractor's bid price. The contract is awarded to the contractor that has the best weighted score. This is also known as a *best value* selection.

- *Qualifications-based selection.* This approach is most often used on design contracts, where the design cost is a small fraction of the construction cost. Increased attention to design can result in large construction savings. Contractors' qualifications are evaluated, the contractors are ranked, and a contract is negotiated with the most qualified firm. If the government and the contractor cannot agree on a reasonable price, the government terminates the negotiations and begins negotiating with the second-ranked firm. Once negotiations are terminated, they cannot be re-opened.

12.1.3 Outputs from Procurement Planning

See Section 12.1.3 of the *PMBOK® Guide* – 2000 Edition.

12.2 SOLICITATION PLANNING

See Section 12.2 of the *PMBOK® Guide* – 2000 Edition.

12.3 SOLICITATION

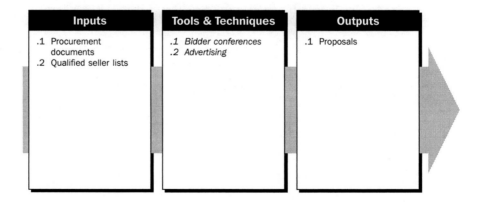

Inputs	Tools & Techniques	Outputs
.1 Procurement documents .2 Qualified seller lists	.1 Bidder conferences .2 Advertising	.1 Proposals

12.3.1 Inputs to Solicitation

See Section 12.3.1 of the *PMBOK® Guide* – 2000 Edition.

12.3.2 Tools and Techniques for Solicitation

Section 12.3.2 of the *PMBOK® Guide* – 2000 Edition discusses tools and techniques for Solicitation. Both are used on government project, but they have particular applications designed to ensure an open competitive process:

.1 Bidder conferences. From the date a procurement document is issued until a determination is made and announced regarding the selection of the contractors, contact between the potential seller and individuals employed by the government is strictly controlled. Specific instructions on communications are generally spelled out in the procurement documents. Once a seller is selected, similar restrictions are in place until the contract is signed. Permissible communication consists of:

■ *Pre-proposal conferences.* If a pre-proposal conference is held, the entire proceeding must be transcribed and provided to every potential bidder. It must be made clear that, in the event of a dispute, the written record is the only admissible evidence. No hearsay or understanding of a verbal comment can be accepted.

■ *Written communication* specifically to clarify questions on the scope statements by the responsible agency.

■ *On-site inspection tours* to offer the bidders a clear understanding of the procurement document requirements that are specified by law. Any statements must be recorded in the same fashion as pre-proposal conferences.

.2 Advertising. To assure an open competition, representative bodies often require that public notices be published in regional publications in the locality of the project. Many governments also publish a bulletin that lists all their contracts that are in the solicitation process. These include the Commerce Business Daily (United States Government), Government Gazette (many governments), California Contracts Register, and similar publications.

12.3.3 Outputs from Solicitation

See Section 12.3.3 of the *PMBOK® Guide* – 2000 Edition.

12.4 SOURCE SELECTION

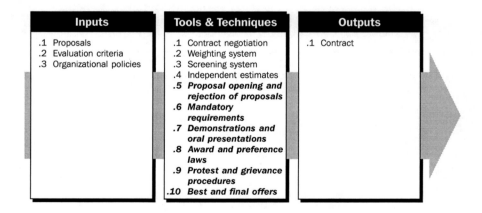

Inputs	Tools & Techniques	Outputs
.1 Proposals	.1 Contract negotiation	.1 Contract
.2 Evaluation criteria	.2 Weighting system	
.3 Organizational policies	.3 Screening system	
	.4 Independent estimates	
	.5 *Proposal opening and rejection of proposals*	
	.6 *Mandatory requirements*	
	.7 *Demonstrations and oral presentations*	
	.8 *Award and preference laws*	
	.9 *Protest and grievance procedures*	
	.10 *Best and final offers*	

12.4.1 Inputs to Source Selection

See Section 12.4.1 of the *PMBOK® Guide* – 2000 Edition.

12.4.2 Tools and Techniques for Source Selection

Section 12.4.2 of the *PMBOK® Guide* – 2000 Edition discusses four tools and techniques for Source Selection. All are used on government projects. Several additional tools are of particular use on government projects:

.1 **Contract negotiation.** See Section 12.4.2.1 of the *PMBOK® Guide* – 2000 Edition.

.2 **Weighting system.** See Section 12.4.2.2 of the *PMBOK® Guide* – 2000 Edition.

.3 **Screening system.** See Section 12.4.2.3 of the *PMBOK® Guide* – 2000 Edition.

.4 **Independent estimates.** See Section 12.4.2.4 of the *PMBOK® Guide* – 2000 Edition.

.5 **Proposal opening and rejection of proposals.** The sealed proposals are publicly opened. The bidders are informed of the time and location of the opening of the proposals. Governments reserve the right to reject any or all proposals received. Proposals become the property of the government. Potential sellers whose proposals are not accepted are notified in writing after the award of the contract.

.6 **Mandatory requirements.** Most contracts have minimum mandatory requirements. The proposals must include evidence that they meet these requirements. Proposals that do not meet the mandatory requirements are excluded from further evaluations. Examples of mandatory requirements include:
   - Compliance with drug-free workplace policy.
   - Format of the proposal.

.7 **Demonstrations and oral presentations.** Demonstrations and presentations are often included as part of the solicitation process. When they are included, they may be either mandatory or optional. Potential sellers demonstrate their proposed package and clarify or explain unusual or significant elements of their proposed package. Potential sellers are not allowed to alter or amend their proposals after submission. Potential sellers are not allowed to conduct negotiations during the interview process. A "best business practice" calls for each panelist to prepare their list of questions so that the same questions are asked of each potential seller.

.8 **Award and preference laws.** Representative bodies often use preferences in procurement to achieve social and economic goals. Preferences may be a percentage weighting or an absolute restriction. Some preferences include:
   - *Regional preference.* In some cases, a resident seller has preference over a non-resident. This preference may be applied by a national government, giving preference to their own nationals, or by a regional or local government, giving preference to regional or local firms.
   - *Population groups.* Governments will often give preference to a particular population group. These may be ethnic groups, people who are deemed to be disadvantaged (e.g., women and disabled people), or people to whom the voters feel indebted (e.g., military veterans). Small business preferences.

.9 **Protest and grievance procedures.** Each governing body has administrative procedures for sellers to file grievances and protests related to an award. Each issue identified by a seller is communicated in writing to the agency. The agency sends a written response to the seller. If the response from the agency has not satisfied the firm, meetings are scheduled. However, final decisions are the agency's responsibility. The seller must exhaust the administrative process before proceeding through the court system.

.10 **Best and final offers.** In some instances, government agencies have the authority to ask the top-rated candidates for "best and final" offers if none of the submitted bids is acceptable as is. When this option is available, it can be a powerful tool for getting a contract more closely meeting an agency's needs.

12.4.3 Outputs from Source Selection

See Section 12.4.3 of the *PMBOK® Guide – 2000 Edition.*

12.5 CONTRACT ADMINISTRATION

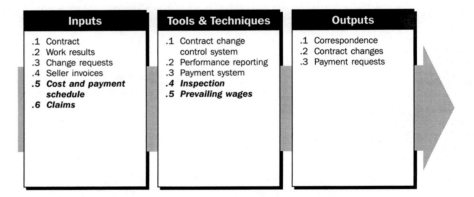

Inputs	Tools & Techniques	Outputs
.1 Contract	.1 Contract change	.1 Correspondence
.2 Work results	control system	.2 Contract changes
.3 Change requests	.2 Performance reporting	.3 Payment requests
.4 Seller invoices	.3 Payment system	
.5 Cost and payment	**.4 Inspection**	
schedule	**.5 Prevailing wages**	
.6 Claims		

12.5.1 Inputs to Contract Administration

Section 12.5.1 of the *PMBOK® Guide – 2000 Edition* discusses four inputs to Contract Administration. All are used on government projects, and two additional tools are of particular use on government projects:

.1 **Contract.** See Section 12.5.1.1 of the *PMBOK® Guide – 2000 Edition.*

.2 **Work results.** See Section 12.5.1.2 of the *PMBOK® Guide – 2000 Edition.*

.3 **Change requests.** See Section 12.5.1.3 of the *PMBOK® Guide – 2000 Edition.*

.4 **Seller invoices.** See Section 12.5.1.4 of the *PMBOK® Guide – 2000 Edition.*

.5 **Cost and payment schedule.** The seller submits progress payment invoices on dates that are specified in the contract. Most government agencies have "prompt payment" rules that require them to pay invoices in a prompt manner.

.6 **Claims.** If the government agency rejects a change requested by the contractor, this creates a potential claim. The project manager is responsible for ensuring the prompt negotiation and settlement of claims. Government agencies generally have a structured dispute resolution process. It can take many years before a final determination is made.

12.5.2 Tools and Techniques for Contract Administration

Section 12.5.2 of the *PMBOK® Guide* – 2000 Edition discusses three tools and techniques for Contract Administration. All are used on government projects, and two additional tools are of particular use on government projects:

.1 Contract change control system. See Section 12.5.2.1 of the *PMBOK® Guide* – 2000 Edition.

.2 Performance reporting. See Section 12.5.2.2 of the *PMBOK® Guide* – 2000 Edition.

.3 Payment system. See Section 12.5.2.3 of the *PMBOK® Guide* – 2000 Edition.

.4 Inspection. Depending on the type of contract, there are various inspection clauses. The government retains the right to inspect project deliverables for compliance to requirements prior to acceptance. The responsible agency has a duty to the voters and taxpayers to ensure that it has received the contracted goods and services, and that these goods and services meet the specifications.

.5 Prevailing wages. Some governments require that contractors pay their employees the prevailing wage. This is the wage paid to the majority of people in the classification on similar projects in the area. If the same wage is not paid to a majority of those in the classification, the prevailing wage is the average of the wages paid. The intent of the prevailing wage requirement is that contractors should win contracts through their management ability, not through cutting the wages of their employees.

12.5.3 Outputs from Contract Administration

See Section 12.5.3 of the *PMBOK® Guide* – 2000 Edition.

12.6 CONTRACT CLOSEOUT

See Section 12.6 of the *PMBOK® Guide* – 2000 Edition.

Appendix A

The Project Management Institute Standards-Setting Process

The Project Management Institute (PMI) Standards-Setting Process was established initially as Institute policy by a vote of the PMI Board of Directors at its October 1993 meeting. In March 1998, the PMI Board of Directors approved modifications to the process. Then in March 1999, it was modified again to make it consistent with the concurrent change in PMI governance procedures.

A.1 PMI STANDARDS DOCUMENTS

PMI Standards Documents are those developed or published by PMI that describe generally accepted practices of project management, specifically:
- *A Guide to the Project Management Body of Knowledge (PMBOK® Guide).*
- Project Management Body of Knowledge Handbooks.

Additional documents may be added to this list by the PMI Standards Manager, subject to the advice and consent of the PMI Project Management Standards Program Member Advisory Group and the PMI Chief Executive Officer. Standards Documents may be original works published by PMI, or they may be publications by other organizations or individuals.

Standards Documents will be developed in accordance with the Code of Good Practice for Standardization developed by the International Organization for Standardization (ISO) and the standards development guidelines established by the American National Standards Institute (ANSI).

A.2 DEVELOPMENT OF ORIGINAL WORKS

Standards Documents that are original works developed by PMI, or revisions of such documents, will be handled as follows:

- Prospective developer(s) will submit a proposal to the PMI Standards Manager. The Manager may also request such proposals. The Manager will submit all received proposals to the PMI Standards Program Member Advisory Group who, with the Manager, will decide whether to accept or reject each proposal.

- The Manager will inform the prospective developer(s) as to the decision and the rationale for the decision. If an approved proposal requires funding in excess of that budgeted for standards development, the Manager will submit the proposal to the PMI Chief Executive Officer for funding.

- For all approved and funded proposals, the Manager will support the developer's efforts so as to maximize the probability that the end product will be accepted. Developer(s) will be required to sign the PMI Volunteer Assignment of Copyright.

- When the proposed material has been completed to the satisfaction of the developer(s), the developer(s) will submit the material to the PMI Standards Manager. The PMI Standards Program Member Advisory Group, with the Manager, will review the proposed material and decide whether to initiate further review by knowledgeable individuals or request additional work by the developer(s).

- The Manager will appoint, subject to review and approval by the PMI Standards Program Member Advisory Group, at least three knowledgeable individuals to review and comment on the material. Based on comments received, the Member Advisory Group will decide whether to accept the material as an exposure draft.

- The PMI Standards Manager will develop a plan for obtaining appropriate public review for each exposure draft. The plan will include a) a review period of not less than one month and not more than six months, b) announcement of the availability of the exposure draft for review in *PMI Today*® (and/or any other similarly appropriate publication media), and c) cost of review copies. The PMI Standards Program Member Advisory Group must approve the Manager's plan for public review. Each exposure draft will include a notice asking for comments to be sent to the PMI Standards Manager at PMI Headquarters and, noting the length of, and expiration date for, the review period.

- Exposure drafts will be published under the aegis of the PMI Publishing Department and must meet the standards of that group regarding typography and style.

- During the review period, the Manager will solicit the formal input of the Managers of other PMI Programs (e.g., Certification, Education, Components, and Publishing) that may be affected by the future publication of the material as a PMI Standard.

- At the conclusion of the review period, the PMI Standards Manager will review comments received with the PMI Standards Program Member Advisory Group, and will work with the developer(s) and others as needed to incorporate appropriate comments. If the comments are major, the PMI Standards Program Member Advisory Group may elect to repeat the exposure draft review process.

- When the PMI Standards Manager and the PMI Standards Program Member Advisory Group have approved a proposed PMI Standards Document, the Manager will promptly submit the document to the PMI Chief

Executive Officer for final review and approval. The PMI Chief Executive Officer will verify compliance with procedures and ensure that member input was sufficient. The PMI Chief Executive Officer will a) approve the document as submitted; b) reject the document; or c) request additional review, and will provide explanatory comments in support of the chosen option.

A.3 ADOPTION OF NON-ORIGINAL WORKS AS STANDARDS

Standards Documents that are the work of other organizations or individuals will be handled as follows:

- Any person or organization may submit a request to the PMI Standards Manager to consider a non-PMI publication as a PMI Standard. The Manager will submit all proposals received to the PMI Standards Program Member Advisory Group who, with the Manager, will decide whether to accept or reject each proposal. If accepted, the Manager will appoint, subject to review and approval by the PMI Standards Program Member Advisory Group, at least three knowledgeable individuals to review and comment on the material.

- During the review period, the Manager will solicit the formal input of the Managers of other PMI Programs (e.g., Certification, Education, Components, and Publishing) that may be affected by the future publication of the material as a PMI Standard.

- Based on comments received, the Member Advisory Group, with the Manager, will decide whether to a) accept the proposal as written as a PMI Standard, b) accept the proposal with modifications and/or an addendum as a PMI Standard, c) seek further review and comment on the proposal (that is, additional reviewers and/or issuance as an exposure draft), or d) reject the proposal. The Manager will inform the submitter as to the decision and the rationale for the decision.

- When the PMI Standards Manager and the PMI Standards Program Member Advisory Group have approved a proposed PMI Standards Document, the Manager will promptly submit the document to the PMI Chief Executive Officer for final review and approval. The Manager will prepare a proposal for the PMI Chief Executive Officer for consideration of a prospective relationship with the owner(s) of the material.

- The PMI Chief Executive Officer will verify compliance with procedures and will ensure that member input was sufficient. The PMI Chief Executive Officer will a) approve the document as submitted; b) reject the document; or c) request additional review, and will provide explanatory comments in support of the chosen option.

Appendix B

Evolution of the Government Extension

In October 1998, the Project Management Institute (PMI) Government Specific Interest Group (SIG) appointed Nigel Blampied as project manager to develop a Government Extension. Over the course of the following year, articles were published in the SIG newsletter both to recruit team members and to begin a discussion on the features that make government projects unique.

A project work breakdown structure was prepared in September 1999; the PMI Standards Member Advisory Group approved a project charter in January 2000 establishing the Government Extension Project as a PMI Standards Project, and appointed Nigel Blampied as the Project Manager.

The team began to assemble in August 1999, mainly in response to articles in the SIG newsletter. Team members are listed in Appendix C. All team members are volunteers, and they come from eight countries. The team includes project managers from all spheres of government—national, regional, and local. They manage projects in several fields, including agriculture, education, energy, health and human services, labor, and transportation.

Each team member was asked to join one or more of the twelve chapter teams, and a lead author was assigned to each chapter. Lead authors were responsible for the successful completion of a particular chapter and wrote the first draft of the chapter. Co-authors contributed ideas and text to the chapter.

Draft 1 of each chapter was submitted to the full team as it was completed. This took place between July and November 2000. Team members responded with 123 recommended amendments. The team evaluated these proposed amendments, approved ninety-one and decided that thirty-two were unpersuasive. Draft 1 with the ninety-one amendments became Draft 2.

In December 2000, Draft 2 was submitted to all members of the Government SIG with known email addresses. SIG members responded with 173 recommended amendments. A core team evaluated these proposed amendments, approved 153 and decided that twenty were unpersuasive. Draft 2 with the 153 amendments became Draft 3.

Draft 3 was submitted to the PMI Standards Program Manager. After a review by the PMI Standards Program Member Advisory Group, the draft was submitted to a panel of Subject Matter Experts (SME) in July, 2001. The panel reviewed the draft, gave it a generally positive review, and recommended that it proceed to the exposure draft. Panel members proposed thirteen specific amendments, and the team incorporated eleven of these into the document. Draft 3 with the eleven amendments became Draft 4, the exposure draft. The PMI Standards Program Member Advisory Group sent the draft and the SME comments back to the team and requested the team consider how to handle each comment and recommendation.

Under the auspices of the PMI Standards Program, PMI published the exposure draft via the PMI Web site on 19 October 2001. Comments were received until 21 December. Ninety-five recommended amendments were submitted. A core team evaluated these proposed amendments, approved sixty-seven, adopted seventeen in a modified form and decided that eleven were unpersuasive. Draft 4 with the eighty-four amendments became the final draft. The project team submitted their final draft to the PMI Standards Manager in March 2002, for review and recommendation by the PMI Standards Program Member Advisory Group to publish as a PMI Standard.

Appendix C

Government Extension Team

PROJECT MANAGER

Nigel Blampied

CHAPTER TEAMS

Each chapter was written by a chapter team, consisting of a lead author and several co-authors. Lead authors were responsible for the successful completion of a particular chapter and wrote the first draft of the chapter. Co-authors contributed ideas and text to the chapter.

Chapter 1: Introduction—Lead Author: Nigel Blampied; Co-authors: Ted Aho, Curt Bramblett, Nicolle Goldman, Ronald Lester, Bongani Matomela, Jack McDaniel, and Roykumar Sukuram.

Chapter 2: Context—Lead Author: Nigel Blampied; Co-authors: Ted Aho, Curt Bramblett, Nicolle Goldman, Ronald Lester, Jack McDaniel, Larry Sieck, and Roykumar Sukuram.

Chapter 3: Processes[28]—Lead Author: Nigel Blampied; Co-authors: Ted Aho, George Belev, Curt Bramblett, Nicolle Goldman, Ronald Lester, and Larry Sieck.

Chapter 4: Project Integration Management—Lead Author: Adrian Hayward; Co-authors: Ted Aho, Nigel Blampied, Curt Bramblett, Dawn Daugherty, Peter Heffron, Jeff Romanczuk, Kazuo Shimizu, Larry Sieck, and Roykumar Sukuram.

Chapter 5: Project Scope Management—Lead Author: Roykumar Sukuram; Co-authors: Ted Aho, Nigel Blampied, Nicolle Goldman, Adrian Hayward, Peter Heffron, Ronald Lester, Linda Salac, and Larry Sieck.

Chapter 6: Project Time Management—Lead Author: Nigel Blampied; Co-authors: Ric Albani, George Belev, Dawn Daugherty, Nicolle Goldman, Ronald Lester, Jack McDaniel, Larry Sieck, and Roykumar Sukuram.

Chapter 7: Project Cost Management—Lead Author: Nigel Blampied; Co-authors: Ted Aho, Curt Bramblett, Nicolle Goldman, Ronald Lester, Jack McDaniel, and Larry Sieck.

Chapter 8: Project Quality Management—Lead Author: Nigel Blampied; Co-authors: Larry Sieck, Roykumar Sukuram, and Dale Woolridge.

Chapter 9: Project Human Resources Management—Lead Author: Dale Woolridge; Co-authors: Ted Aho, Nigel Blampied, Curt Bramblett, Dawn Daugherty, and Larry Sieck.

Chapter 10: Project Communications Management—Lead Author: Jeff Romanczuk; Co-authors: Emmanuel Abégunrin, Nigel Blampied, Curt Bramblett, Nicolle Goldman, Jack McDaniel, and Larry Sieck.

Chapter 11: Project Risk Management—Lead Author: Nigel Blampied; Co-authors: Ted Aho, Nicolle Goldman, Ronald Lester, Larry Sieck, Roykumar Sukuram, and Dale Woolridge.

Chapter 12: Project Procurement Management—Lead Authors: Dawn Daugherty and Linda Salac; Co-authors: Ted Aho, Nigel Blampied, Nicolle Goldman, Adrian Hayward, Ronald Lester, Jack McDaniel, James McGee, Bradley Poeckes, Steven Schafer, and Larry Sieck.

TEAM MEMBER AFFILIATIONS

- Emmanuel A. Abégunrin, MBA, Canada
- Ted Aho, PMP, USA
- Ric Albani, PMP, USA
- George Belev, USA
- Nigel Blampied, P.E., PMP, USA
- Curt P. Bramblett, PMP, USA
- Dawn Daugherty, PMP, USA
- Nicolle Goldman, PMP, USA
- Adrian Hayward, United Kingdom
- Peter Heffron, USA
- Vicente Cordero Herrera, Mexico
- Ronald Lester, USA
- Rodrigo Loureiro, PMP, Brazil
- Bongani Matomela, South Africa
- Jack McDaniel, MBA, CGFM, USA
- James McGee, USA
- Takeshi Nishi, Japan
- Bradley Poeckes, PMP, USA
- Jeff Romanczuk, PMP, USA
- Linda Salac, USA
- Steven Schafer, USA
- Kazuo Shimizu, PMP, Japan
- Larry Sieck, USA
- Roykumar Sukuram, PMP, South Africa
- Dale Woolridge, Ph.D., USA
- Carlos R. Zervigón, PMP, USA

DRAFT 1 AMENDMENT EVALUATORS

Draft 1 of each chapter was submitted to the full team. Team members responded with 123 recommended amendments. The team evaluated these proposed amendments, approved ninety-one and decided that thirty-two were unpersuasive. Once the ninety-one amendments were made to Draft 1, it became Draft 2. Evaluators of the amendments were Nigel Blampied, Curt Bramblett, Dawn Daugherty, Nicolle Goldman, Adrian Hayward, Peter Heffron, Jack McDaniel, Jeff Romanczuk, Kazuo Shimizu, and Dale Woolridge.

DRAFT 2 AMENDMENT EVALUATORS

Draft 2 was submitted to all members of the Government SIG with known email addresses. SIG members responded with 173 recommended amendments. Six team members evaluated these proposed amendments, approved 153 and decided that twenty were unpersuasive. Once the 153 amendments were made to Draft 2, it became Draft 3. The six evaluators were Emmanuel Abégunrin, Nigel Blampied, Curt Bramblett, Nicolle Goldman, Adrian Hayward, and Linda Salac.

SELECTED REVIEWERS OF PRE-EXPOSURE DRAFT

These volunteers provided specific evaluations and comments on the pre-exposure draft. The project team and the PMI Standards Program Team considered their input in the development of the Exposure Draft.
- Raymond Abé, MPD, Australia
- Michael Airaudi, PMP, USA
- William Bahnmaier, PMP, USA
- Brenda Breslin, PMP, USA
- Edward Commons, PMP, USA
- Peter Sheremeta, Canada
- Carel Van Zyl, PMP, South Africa
- Aloysio Vianna, Jr., PMP, Brazil

RESPONDENTS TO PRE-EXPOSURE DRAFT REVIEW

Reviewers of the pre-exposure draft proposed thirteen specific amendments. Nine team members evaluated these proposed amendments and incorporated eleven of them into the document; the other two were deemed unpersuasive. The nine evaluators were Emmanuel Abégunrin, Ted Aho, Nigel Blampied, Nicolle Goldman, Peter Heffron, Jack McDaniel, Jeff Romanczuk, Linda Salac, and Larry Sieck.

REVIEWERS OF EXPOSURE DRAFT

In addition to team members and pre-exposure draft reviewers, the following individuals provided comments on the exposure draft of this document:
- David Drevinsky, P.E., PMP, USA
- Bruce A. Geanaros, USA
- Paul Lawrey, PMP, USA
- Tess Mulrooney, USA
- Francis O'Brien, PMP, USA
- George Sukumar, P.E., USA
- Judy L. Van Meter, USA

RESPONDENTS TO EXPOSURE DRAFT REVIEW

Reviewers of the exposure draft proposed ninety-five amendments. Twelve team members evaluated these proposed amendments and incorporated seventy-four of them into the document. The twelve evaluators were Raymond Abé, Emmanuel Abégunrin, Ted Aho, Nigel Blampied, Brenda Breslin, Nicolle Goldman, Adrian Hayward, Peter Heffron, Jeff Romanczuk, Linda Salac, Larry Sieck, and Carel Van Zyl.

PMI STANDARDS PROGRAM MEMBER ADVISORY GROUP 2001-2002

- Sergio R. Coronado, Spain
- J. Brian Hobbs, PMP, Canada
- Tom Kurihara, USA
- Bobbye S. Underwood, PMP, USA
- Julia M. Bednar, PMP, USA
- George Beleve, USA
- Cynthia A. Berg, PMP, USA

PMI HEADQUARTERS STAFF

- Steven L. Fahrenkrog, PMP, PMI Standards Manager
- Kristin L. Wright, PMI Standards Program Administrator
- Iesha Brown, PMI Certification Program Administrator
- Eva Goldman, PMI Technical Research Standards Associate
- Linda Cherry, PMI Publisher
- Richard Schwartz, PMI Book Development Editor
- Danielle Moore, PMI Book Publishing Planner

Appendix D

Notes

[1] Project Management Institute. 2000. *A Guide to the Project Management Body of Knowledge (PMBOK® Guide) – 2000 Edition*. Newtown Square, Pa.: Project Management Institute.

[2] See Section 1.1 of *A Guide to the Project Management Body of Knowledge (PMBOK® Guide) – 2000 Edition* for the definition of "generally accepted."

[3] Project Management Institute. 2000. *A Guide to the Project Management Body of Knowledge (PMBOK® Guide) – 2000 Edition*. Newtown Square, Pa.: Project Management Institute, page 3.

[4] Project Management Institute. 2000. *A Guide to the Project Management Body of Knowledge (PMBOK® Guide) – 2000 Edition*. Newtown Square, Pa.: Project Management Institute, page 181.

[5] In some cases, the taxes are deferred by using bonds to fund projects. Over time, the bonds are paid off by taxes and fees.

[6] This principle dates back at least to the Magna Carta and, in some countries, probably earlier. Article 12 of the Magna Carta, signed in 1215 by King John of England, says, "No scutage or aid shall be imposed in our realm unless by the common counsel of our realm."

[7] This is true even if the project manager works in the legislative branch of a government (e.g., the project manager may be responsible for managing audits for the legislative branch). Within the legislative branch, there are executive officers responsible for day-to-day operations. The project manager would be part of this executive-within-the-legislature.

[8] Such abuses are most likely in places where there are severe limitations on voting rights (most often limitations based on ethnicity or length of residence).

[9] Project Management Institute. 2000. *A Guide to the Project Management Body of Knowledge (PMBOK® Guide) – 2000 Edition*. Newtown Square, Pa.: Project Management Institute, page 10. This definition is quoted from Turner, J. Rodney. 1992. *The Handbook of Project-Based Management*. New York, N.Y.: McGraw-Hill.

[10] Project Management Institute. 2000. *A Guide to the Project Management Body of Knowledge (PMBOK® Guide) – 2000 Edition*. Newtown Square, Pa.: Project Management Institute, page 11.

[11] Project Management Institute. 2000. *A Guide to the Project Management Body of Knowledge (PMBOK® Guide) – 2000 Edition*. Newtown Square, Pa.: Project Management Institute, page 16.

[12] Project Management Institute. 2000. *A Guide to the Project Management Body of Knowledge (PMBOK® Guide) – 2000 Edition*. Newtown Square, Pa.: Project Management Institute, page 30.

[13] Project Management Institute. 2000. *A Guide to the Project Management Body of Knowledge (PMBOK® Guide)* – 2000 Edition. Newtown Square, Pa.: Project Management Institute, page 41.

[14] Project Management Institute. 2000. *A Guide to the Project Management Body of Knowledge (PMBOK® Guide)* – 2000 Edition. Newtown Square, Pa.: Project Management Institute, page 51.

[15] Project Management Institute. 2000. *A Guide to the Project Management Body of Knowledge (PMBOK® Guide)* – 2000 Edition. Newtown Square, Pa.: Project Management Institute, page 53.

[16] Project Management Institute. 2000. *A Guide to the Project Management Body of Knowledge (PMBOK® Guide)* – 2000 Edition. Newtown Square, Pa.: Project Management Institute, page 65.

[17] For countries that use English law, the annual budget originates from the English Declaration of Rights. William III and Mary II signed this in 1689. It prevented the king from maintaining an army without the consent of Parliament. Its goal was to prevent the king from using the army against the people, as Charles I had done in the Civil War. Parliament began to pass six-month "Mutiny Acts" to permit the king to keep his army. They were later changed to annual acts.

The United States adopted a version of the British limit. Article 1, Section 8 of the U.S. Constitution says that, "[The congress shall have power] to raise and support armies, but no appropriation of money for that use shall be for a longer term than two years." Article 1, Section 9 adds, "No money shall be drawn from the treasury, but in consequences of appropriation made by law."

[18] Project Management Institute. 2000. *A Guide to the Project Management Body of Knowledge (PMBOK® Guide)* – 2000 Edition. Newtown Square, Pa.: Project Management Institute, page 83.

[19] Project Management Institute. 2000. *A Guide to the Project Management Body of Knowledge (PMBOK® Guide)* – 2000 Edition. Newtown Square, Pa.: Project Management Institute, page 95.

[20] Project Management Institute. 2000. *A Guide to the Project Management Body of Knowledge (PMBOK® Guide)* – 2000 Edition. Newtown Square, Pa.: Project Management Institute, page 98. This is a quotation from the International Organization for Standardization. ISO 8402. 1994. *Quality Management and Quality Assurance.* Geneva, Switzerland: ISO Press.

[21] Project Management Institute. 2000. *A Guide to the Project Management Body of Knowledge (PMBOK® Guide)* – 2000 Edition. Newtown Square, Pa.: Project Management Institute, page 98.

[22] Project Management Institute. 2000. *A Guide to the Project Management Body of Knowledge (PMBOK® Guide)* – 2000 Edition. Newtown Square, Pa.: Project Management Institute, page 107.

[23] Project Management Institute. 2000. *A Guide to the Project Management Body of Knowledge (PMBOK® Guide)* – 2000 Edition. Newtown Square, Pa.: Project Management Institute, page 117.

[24] Project Management Institute. 2000. *A Guide to the Project Management Body of Knowledge (PMBOK® Guide)* – 2000 Edition. Newtown Square, Pa.: Project Management Institute, page 127.

[25] Project Management Institute. 2000. *A Guide to the Project Management Body of Knowledge (PMBOK® Guide)* – 2000 Edition. Newtown Square, Pa.: Project Management Institute, page 147.

[26] ENR (Engineering News Record). 2000. July 24/July 31, page 51.

[27] W. Edwards Deming. 2000. *Out of the Crisis.* Cambridge, Mass.: The MIT Press, page 23. (Originally published: Cambridge, Mass.: MIT, Center for Advanced Educational Services, 1986.)

[28] Although Chapter 3 is very brief, several proposals were considered for this chapter before the team decided to adopt the current brief text.

Appendix E

Application Area Extensions

E.1 NEED FOR APPLICATION AREA EXTENSIONS

Application area extensions are necessary when there are generally accepted knowledge and practices for a category of projects in one application area that are not generally accepted across the full range of project types in most application areas. Application area extensions reflect:

- Unique or unusual aspects of the project environment that the project management team must be aware of in order to manage the project efficiently and effectively.
- Common knowledge and practices which, if followed, will improve the efficiency and effectiveness of the project (e.g., standard work breakdown structures).

Application area-specific knowledge and practices can arise as a result of many factors, including, but not limited to, differences in cultural norms, technical terminology, societal impact, or project life cycles. For example:

- In construction, where virtually all work is accomplished under contract, there are common knowledge and practices related to procurement that do not apply to all categories of projects.
- In bioscience, there are common knowledge and practices driven by the regulatory environment that do not apply to all categories of projects.
- In government contracting, there are common knowledge and practices driven by government acquisition regulations that do not apply to all categories of projects.
- In consulting, there are common knowledge and practices created by the project manager's sales and marketing responsibilities that do not apply to all categories of projects.

Application area extensions are:

- *Additions* to the core material of Chapters 1 through 12 of the *PMBOK® Guide* – 2000 Edition, *not substitutes* for it.
- Organized in a fashion similar to the *PMBOK® Guide* – 2000 Edition; that is, by identifying and describing the project management processes unique to that application area.

■ Unique additions to the core material such as:
  ◆ Identifying new or modified processes
  ◆ Subdividing existing processes
  ◆ Describing different sequences or interactions of processes
  ◆ Increasing elements to or modifying the common process definitions
  ◆ Defining special inputs, tools and techniques and/or outputs for the existing processes.

Application area extensions are *not*:

■ "How to" documents or "practice guidelines"—such documents may be issued as PMI Standards, but they are not what are intended as extensions

■ A lower level of detail than is addressed in this document—such details may be addressed in handbooks or guidebooks which may be issued as PMI Standards, but they are not what is intended as extensions.

E.2 CRITERIA FOR DEVELOPMENT OF APPLICATION AREA EXTENSIONS

Extensions will be developed under the following criteria:

■ There is a substantial body of knowledge that is both project-oriented and unique, or nearly unique to that application area.

■ There is an identifiable PMI component (e.g., a PMI Specific Interest Group, College or a Chapter), or an identifiable external organization willing and able to commit the necessary resources to subscribe to and support the PMI Standards Program with the development and maintenance of a specific PMI Standard. Or, the extension may be developed by PMI itself.

■ The proposed extension is able to pass the same level of rigorous PMI Project Management Standard-Setting Process as any other PMI Standard.

E.3 PUBLISHING AND FORMAT OF APPLICATION AREA EXTENSIONS

Application area extensions are developed and/or published by PMI, or they are developed and/or published by either a PMI component or by an external organization under a formal agreement with PMI.

■ Extensions match the *PMBOK® Guide* – 2000 Edition in style and content. They use the paragraph and subparagraph numbers of the *PMBOK® Guide* – 2000 Edition for the material that has been extended.

■ Sections and paragraphs of the *PMBOK® Guide* – 2000 Edition that are not extended are not repeated in extensions.

■ Extensions contain a rationale/justification about the need for an extension and its material.

■ Extensions are delimited in terms of what they are *not* intended to do.

E.4 PROCESS FOR DEVELOPMENT AND MAINTENANCE OF APPLICATION AREA EXTENSIONS

When approved in accord with the PMI Standards-Setting Process, Application area extensions become PMI Standards. They will be developed and maintained in accordance with the process described below.

■ An extension must be sponsored by PMI, a formally chartered PMI component (e.g., a Specific Interest Group, College or a Chapter), or another organization external to PMI, which has been approved by the PMI Standards Program Member Advisory Group and the PMI Standards Program Manager. Co-sponsorship with PMI is the preferred arrangement. All approvals will be by formal written agreement between PMI and the sponsoring entity, which agreement will include, among other things, the parties' agreement as to intellectual property ownership rights and publications rights to the extension.

■ A project to develop, publish and/or maintain an extension must be approved by the PMI Standards Program. Permission to initiate, develop and maintain an extension must be received from PMI, and will be the subject of an agreement between or among the organizations. If there is no other sponsoring organization, the PMI Standards Program may elect to proceed alone.

■ The sponsoring group will notify and solicit advice and support from the PMI Standards Program Member Advisory Group and PMI Standards Program Manager throughout the development and maintenance process. They will concur with the appropriateness of the sponsoring organization for the extension proposed and will review the extension during its development to identify any conflicts or overlaps with other similar projects that may be under way.

■ The sponsoring group will prepare a proposal to develop the extension. The proposal will include a justification for the project with a matrix of application-area-specific processes and the affected sections of this document. It will also contain the commitment of sufficient qualified drafters and reviewers; identification of funding requirements, including reproduction, postage, telephone costs, desktop publishing, etc.; commitment to the PMI procedures for PMI Standards extension development and maintenance; and a plan and schedule for same.

■ Following acceptance of the proposal, the project team will prepare a project charter for approval by the sponsoring group and the PMI Standards Program Team. The charter will include sources of funding and any funding proposed to be provided by PMI. It will include a requirement for periodic review of the extension with reports to the PMI Standards Program Team and a "Sunset Clause" that specifies when, and under what conditions, the extension will be removed from active status as a PMI Standard.

■ The proposal will be submitted to the PMI Standards Manager in accordance with the PMI Standards-Setting Process. The PMI Standards Manager will determine if the proposal can be expected to result in a document that will meet the requirements for a PMI Standard, and if adequate resources and sources of support have been identified. To help with this determination, the PMI Standards Manager will seek review and comment by the PMI Standards Program Member Advisory Group and, if appropriate, a panel of knowledgeable persons not involved with the extension.

■ The PMI Standards Manager, with the support of the PMI Standards Program Member Advisory Group, will monitor and support the development of the approved project. A project charter must be approved by the sponsoring organization(s) and by the PMI Standards Program Team.

■ The sponsoring organization will develop the extension according to the approved project charter, including coordinating with the PMI Standards Program Team for support, review and comment.

■ When the extension has been completed to the satisfaction of the sponsoring organization, it will be submitted to the PMI Standards Manager, who will manage the final approval and publication processes in accordance with the PMI Standards-Setting Process. This final submittal will include listing of and commitment by the sponsoring organization to the PMI extension maintenance processes and efforts.

■ Following approval of the extension as a PMI Standard, the sponsoring organization will implement the extension maintenance process in accordance with the approved plan.

Glossary

Best Value Selection. See *Weighted Price and Qualifications*.

Civil Service System. A system in which government employees hold office from one administration to another. Their positions are protected provided that they remain politically neutral. See *Spoils System*.

Constructive Demotion. Assigning a civil servant to a position that is perceived to be inferior.

Defined Contribution. Split funding by program where some programs contribute a fixed amount, with one program funding the balance.

Defined Elements of Work. Split funding by program where each program bears the cost of its portion(s) of the project.

Devolution. Delegation of work or power by a national government to a regional or local government; or by a regional government to a local government.

Devolve. See *Devolution*.

Eminent Domain. A process that allows the government to take possession of private property when this is deemed to be in the best interests of the public.

Encumbrance. See *Obligation*.

Full and Open Competition After Exclusion of Sources. A process in which agencies are allowed to exclude one or more sources from competing for a contract. A set-aside for small businesses or small disadvantaged firms is an example of this method.

Full and Open Competition. A process in which all responsible sources are allowed to compete for a contract.

Government Transfer Payment. See *Obligation*.

Hybrid Staff. A mixture of civil service and contracted staff.

Indefinite Delivery Indefinite Quantity Contracts (IDIQ). Contracts that state the type of service to be delivered, give a length of time in which the service can be requested (generally five years), and specify the minimum and maximum contract amount, but no specific project information.

Line-Item Projects. Projects which are added to the budget by the representative body on a project-by-project basis.

Local Government. The government of a small portion of a country or region. There are often overlapping local governments with different duties. Local governments include counties, cities, towns, municipalities, school boards, water boards, road boards, sanitation districts, electrification districts, fire protection districts, and hospital districts. They are governed by elected boards. This election distinguishes them from local branches of regional or national governments.

Lowest Qualified Bidder. A contracting process in which the lowest bid is accepted. Contractors' proposals are evaluated to ensure that they meet minimum qualifications. The level of qualification may vary. On construction contracts, the minimum qualification is generally a contractor's license and a performance bond. On professional service contracts, there is generally a more detailed evaluation of the contractors' qualifications.

Matching Funds. A form of split funding by program. When governments "devolve" project selection to lower representative bodies, they often require those lower bodies to pay a portion of the project cost. Matching funds may be apportioned on a percentage basis or as a defined contribution.

Multiple Award Schedules. A contracting process sometimes used when there is a generally accepted "reasonable price" for a good or service. Contractors submit their schedule of rates to the government procurement office. If these are approved, government agencies may buy goods and services at the published rates without a separate competition.

National Government. The government of an internationally recognized country. The country may be a confederation, federation, or unitary state.

Obligation. A process that places funds for a contract into a separate account that can be used only for the specific contract. The funds remain available for two to five years, depending on the rules set by the representative body. This avoids the need to vote funds in each fiscal year.

On-Call Contracts. See *Indefinite Delivery Indefinite Quantity Contracts*.

Opposition Stakeholders. Stakeholders who perceive themselves as being harmed if the project is successful.

Other Than Full and Open Competition. A process in which there is only a single contractor that can accomplish the work, by reason of experience, possession of specialized facilities, or technical competence, in a time frame required by the government.

Percentage Split. Split funding by program where each program funds a percentage of the project.

Prevailing Wage. The wage paid to the majority of the people in a classification on similar projects in the area. If the same wage is not paid to a majority of those in the classification, the prevailing wage is the average of the wages paid.

Program. A group of projects managed in a coordinated way to obtain benefits not available from managing them individually.

Qualifications-Based Selection. A contracting process in which the contract is awarded to the contractor that is best qualified among those that offer a price that is reasonable to the government. This approach is most often used on design contracts, where the design cost is a small fraction of the construction cost. Increased attention to design can result in large construction savings. Contractors' qualifications are evaluated, the contractors are ranked, and a contract is negotiated with the most qualified firm. If the government and the contractor cannot agree on a reasonable price, the government terminates the negotiations and begins negotiating with the second-ranked firm. Once negotiations are terminated they cannot be re-opened.

Regional Government. The government of a portion of a large country. In small countries, there are no regional governments—only a national government and local governments. In confederations and federations, the regional government has considerable autonomy. In unitary states, the regional government is subject to control by the national government. Regions are called by many different terms. These terms include states, provinces, lander, departments, cantons, kingdoms, principalities, republics, regions, and territories.

Regulators. The individuals or organizations that must approve various aspects of the project. Regulators enforce rules and regulations. They are actively involved in the project, but they generally have no interest in its success—it will not affect them. Regulators are either agents of a higher government or of another agency in the same government as the performing organization.

Representative Body. A group of people, elected by the voters, who meet, deliberate, and set rules. They may call these rules by several names. They include laws, statutes, ordinances, regulations, and policies.

Sole Source Contract. See *Other Than Full and Open Competition*.

Split Funding by Fiscal Year. The process of funding a single project from more than one annual budget.

Split Funding by Program. The process of funding a single project from more than one program.

Spoils System. A system in which each new administration can replace government employees. See *Civil Service System*.

Tight Matrix. A system in which each project has an assigned work area, and employees sit together in that area while they are working on the project, even though they do not report to the same supervisor.

Triple Constraint. A relationship between product scope, time, and cost. If a change is made to any of the three factors, at least one other factor must change.

Use It or Lose It. Provisions in an annual budget that require funds to be spent, or obligated, by the end of the fiscal year.

Weighted Price and Qualifications. A contracting process in which contractors are evaluated against several factors, with a pre-determined weight assigned to each factor. A weight is also assigned to the contractor's bid price. The contract is awarded to the contractor that has the best weighted score.

Index

A

acceptance 52, 63, 79
accounting 28, 30
activity attributes 25
activity duration estimates 24
additional planning 17
administrative closure 43
advertising 60
affirmative action 46, 48
agency policy or law 43
air and water quality 46, 48
annual budget 30, 32, 76, 82–83
annual budget cycle 24–25, 28–29, 32
application area 1, 2, 77–79
appraisals 37
approval controls 14
assumptions 14, 21, 24, 40, 57
assumptions analysis 48
Australia 4, 73
avoidance 14, 52
award and preference laws 61

B

basic planning report 8
benchmarking 32
benefit/cost analysis 32
best and final offers 62
best practices 50
best value 56–57, 59, 81
bid 8, 59, 81, 83
bidder conferences 60
brainstorming 48
Brazil 4, 73
budget 3, 8, 20, 24–25, 27, 29, 32, 36, 81. *See also* annual budget cycle, annual budget
budget proposal 8
bureaucracy 40
business need 20

C

calendars 24
Canada 4, 73–74
chancellor 4
change control system 16
change requests 16, 42, 62
charter 21, 79
checklists 48
chief executive 3, 32, 65–67
CITES. *See* Convention on International Trade in Endangered Species (CITES)
cities 5, 81
citizen 2
civil servants 36, 55
civil service 14, 36–38
civil service flexibility 37
civil service system 36, 81, 83
claims 62
closing processes 11
Code Napoleon 58
coding structure 25
committee 3
communication management plan 15
communications management plan 41
communications planning 40
communications requirements 40
communications technology 40
competitive process 56–57, 60
configuration management 16
conflicts of interest 56
constituent 20–21, 40, 55
constraints 14, 21, 24–25, 36, 40, 57
constructive demotion 36, 81
consultants 40, 42
contingency reserve 52
contract 15–16, 25, 28, 30, 37, 55, 58–60
contract change control system 63
contract negotiation 61
contract type selection 57

For Additional PMI Titles, Please Visit and
Shop Our Online Bookstore at ***www.pmibookstore.org***

Book Ordering Information

Phone: toll-free 1-866-276-4PMI (within U.S.)
          1-770-280-4129 (outside the U.S.)
Fax: 1-770-280-4148
Email: pmiorders@pbd.com
Mail: PMI Publications Fulfillment Center
         PO Box 932683
         Atlanta, GA 31193-2683 USA

Visit PMI's website at www.pmi.org